the world is your oracle

Quarto is the authority on a wide range of topics.

Quarto educates, entertains and enriches the lives of our readers—enthusiasts and lovers of hands-on living.

www.QuartoKnows.com

© 2017 Quarto Publishing Group USA Inc.
Text © 2017 Nancy Vedder-Shults

First published in the United States of America in 2017 by
Fair Winds Press, an imprint of
Quarto Publishing Group USA Inc.
100 Cummings Center, Suite 406-L
Beverly, Massachusetts 01915-6101
Telephone: (978) 282-9590 | Fax: (978) 283-2742
QuartoKnows.com
Visit our blogs at QuartoKnows.com

21 20 19 18 17   1 2 3 4 5

ISBN: 978-1-59233-757-6

Library of Congress Cataloging-in-Publication Data
Vedder-Shults, Nancy, author.
The world is your oracle : divinatory practices for tapping your inner
  wisdom and getting the answers you need / Nancy Vedder-Shults, Ph.D.
ISBN 9781592337576 (softbound)
1. Divination. 2. Oracles.
BF1745 .V43 2017
133.3--dc23
2016035414

Design and Page Layout: Stacy Wakefield Forte
Cover Image: Linnea Vedder
Illustration: Linnea Vedder

Printed in China

MIX
Paper from
responsible sources
FSC® C016973

*to the touchstone circle and my dream
group, who nudged me gently out of my
head and into my body-mind-spirit.*

CONTENTS

INTRODUCTION

what's an oracle?

FROM THE ANCIENT GREEKS to modern-day North Americans, people from cultures all over the globe have gained insight into many questions by using oracles. These divinatory practices have been performed at times when significant decisions needed to be made: to establish new capital cities, to choose religious leaders, to create inventions, to dig wells, to write poetry, and to compose music. But more importantly, they can help you in your daily life to stay happy and healthy.

First, what are oracles? An oracle is simply a technique for uncovering an answer to a question. If you're stumped by a situation—or by the behavior of a person—in your life, an oracle can help you understand the problem. If you can't figure out how to proceed when it comes to crucial decisions at work or at home, an oracle can give you advice. These divinatory practices reveal guideposts for your life by helping you to tap into your unconscious mind, where your inner wisdom resides. After all, your conscious, analytical mind only has access to the tip of the iceberg when it comes to your thoughts and your experience, but your unconscious contains much more below the surface of your day-to-day mindset. It's a storehouse of hunches, feelings, instincts, and all sorts of knowledge that you can access through divination. It's the fount of your memories, your creativity, and your intuitions.

You've probably heard of tarot cards or the *I Ching*. Maybe a friend has even offered to cast runes for you. All of these are oracles or divinatory practices. But unlike the methods in this book, they use preprogrammed answers for the questions you bring to them. The techniques in *The World Is Your Oracle* are different. They will help you tune in to your inner depths by employing the three major intuitive senses: the auditory, visual, and kinesthetic. Depending on how your mind works, one of these will unlock the mysterious realm of intuition in your depths (see chapter 1, p. 22).

THE THREE MAJOR INTUITIVE SENSES

- **VISUAL.** If you tend to be visually oriented, the divinations here will help you develop your "second sight"—with techniques like scrying, dream incubation, or balloon diagrams (see chapter 3 for visual divinations).

- **AUDITORY.** If hearing affects you most, you'll find techniques in this book for listening to the "still, small voice within"—like chanting, listening to birdsong, or asking an ancestor for advice (see chapter 4 for auditory oracles).

- **KINESTHETIC.** If touch nurtures you or if you're always in motion, the oracles here will connect you with your "body wisdom" or "gut feelings"—through journaling, using a mudra, or sculpting clay (see chapter 5 for kinesthetic oracles).

how oracles foster wisdom in your life

EVERY DAY, WE'RE BOMBARDED by advertising messages, expert advice, campaign promises, and opinions of every sort. Sometimes it's hard to hear ourselves think. Instead, we need to listen to what Apple CEO and co-founder Steve Jobs called "the whisperings" of intuition. According to Jobs, these wise flashes of inspiration will help us to be successful in an environment of rapid change, where analytical thinking no longer suffices. In fact, a gathering of 1,500 corporate CEOs from around the world recently identified creative insight as the best strategy for dealing with a world that is volatile, uncertain, and complex.[1]

Recent studies also show that to a large degree we reach our decisions unconsciously.[2] Our unconscious mind constantly monitors our external and internal environments, and when it judges the information gathered to be important enough, it engages the conscious mind, and we become "consciously aware" of something. Oracles can put us in touch with our unconscious wisdom sooner, so we don't have to wait out those times when our analytical mind is stuck in a rut.

On a more personal level, I've found that a good oracle puts you in touch with yourself. It lets you discover your motivations, feelings, and thoughts about any question you're exploring. It also helps by alerting you to your hidden wishes and fears—those aspects of your personality that might sabotage your conscious choices unless you take them into account. Once you're aware of the beliefs that are operating beneath the surface of your mind, you can factor them into your decisions, just like any conscious thought.

Oracles can guide your life with a sure hand when you flounder. They can help you set priorities, meet challenges, and find creative solutions to your problems. At times, a divination can even point to an outworn habit that you need to discard, or can encourage you to take a risk that you might have been too timid to tackle on your own. Oracles can provide information that you need, warn you of possible dangers, and inspire your professional and creative work.

everything comes alive

FINALLY, I THINK WE ALL long to be touched by something greater than ourselves, and divination provides that experience. In fact, the word itself derives from the Latin *divi*, meaning "deity," implying that oracles connect us with the sacred. I believe that just as childhood play prepares a person for adulthood, so, too, the "play" of divination prepares a person for a life of sacred encounters. In performing oracles, we acquire practice in inviting the touch of the ineffable, a discipline that can carry over into our lives.

The ultimate aim of divination is exactly that: to help us get back in touch with the sacred within us and around us, to open us up to a sense of wonder. Our lives can be imbued with a richer significance as a result of being brushed by the mystery of divination as we experience ourselves in relation to something larger than our routine lives. It can create an ongoing awareness of the adventure of our lives, open at any moment to our inner knowing and the wisdom of the universe.

As my friend Rue Hass says in her book *This Is Where I Stand*, "The wonderful thing about using the world as my oracle is that I become acutely aware of my presence in it, and my relationship to everything. *Everything comes alive!*"[3] It is my hope that you, too, will be inspired, delighted, and illuminated through the techniques in the chapters that follow.

1

PREPARING,

INTERPRETING,

AND HONORING

YOUR ORACLE

THE WORLD IS YOUR ORACLE invites you to tap into your inner wisdom in a variety of ways. For instance, you can read the patterns in the stars. You can listen to a fire sing as it burns. You can flip open a book and read the first phrase that catches your eye. While writing this book, I opened a nearby volume and read, "Listen to the cry of your own heart. Something wonderful is being said."[4]

If you're new to divination, welcome. You'll learn to connect with your own heart's cry with strategies for a successful oracle, from creating a favorable atmosphere, to constructing your question, to interpreting your divination. If you're familiar with divination, you'll encounter oracular methods that will expand your intuitive skills and respond to your questions in greater depth.

Whether you're new to divination or an experienced practitioner, the divinations gathered here will help you to find your own insight, answer your own questions, and know your own truth. And along the way, you may also develop sharper perceptions, deepen your curiosity about each day's small miracles, experience a greater sense of wonder, and be more confident in your personal choices.

first, find the question

IT'S USUALLY A GOOD IDEA to devise your question before choosing an oracle and performing the divination. I've learned this from experience: Over the years, I've come to value my questions as much as the answers to them. Questions can create possibilities, freedom, and choices—especially if you don't limit the truth that you're willing to hear. In fact, a question can guide you just as surely as a response to that query. So, when you're considering a divination question, keep these things in mind:

STAY OPEN TO INTUITION. When developing a divination question, it's important to stay open to possibility. Try not to shut down your intuition too soon: Restricting the range of your request often inhibits your inner wisdom. That means it's best to avoid "who" or "where" questions. They don't allow your unconscious enough room to play. Plus, the answers to such questions tend to be too specific and provide little insight. In contrast, "why" questions tend to be too broad and can yield philosophical answers that give you little practical guidance. Open-ended questions like these may provide answers that are too vague. That's why it's best to use specific "what" and "how" questions, which will usually give you the information you need. Don't stress too much if this is the first time you've created a divination question. Experience is the best teacher: After crafting a number of divinatory queries, you'll begin to know what kind of question works best for you.

LET GO OF PRECONCEPTIONS. People often know what they want to hear from an oracle, so they fashion a leading question that results in the desired answer. For example, instead of asking "Does Bill love me?" a person might ask, "How much does Bill love me?" The second question assumes that Bill loves the querent—which is, of course, exactly what he or she wants to hear. To avoid this common mistake, it's important to let go of the assumptions you've made about your issue and to surrender to the power of the messages you receive. Relinquishing control in this way can feel scary at first, but by doing so, you'll gain the precious wisdom available from the mysterious realm of insight within you.

RESPECT THE ORACLE. If you find yourself asking the same question over and over again, you may be attempting to influence the outcome of your divination. If you don't like the first oracle you receive, for instance, and you continue to ask until you finally hear or see what you want, you're probably trying to manipulate the result of your divination. Avoid this; such duplication of effort can actually weaken the purpose of an oracle.

For this reason, follow-up questions can be tricky. In most cases, it's best to avoid them. But once you're having a conversation—with an **Ancestor**, during **Divine Inspiration**, **Guided Meditation**, or possibly **Intuition**—you may need to ask for clarification. It's important that additional questions don't restate your query in different words, but instead look deeper into the implications of the answer you've already received. Try using a general follow-up like "Tell me more!" or "Can you explain?" Or, ask for more information by using an open-ended question, which hands over control of the conversation to your inner wisdom.

RESPECT BOUNDARIES. Unless you're undertaking a divination for a friend, limit your questions about others to your relationship with them. Only rarely will you receive direct information about someone other than yourself. Even if you ask a question about someone else, your oracle is more likely to tell you about your relationship with that person instead. Characters who appear in your dreams or oracles almost always reflect some aspect of yourself or your connection with the individual involved.

NOT EVERY ANSWER NEEDS A QUESTION. Oracles exist everywhere. If you're receptive to them and trust them to guide you toward the depths of your wisdom, you may not need to ask a specific question. Instead, you can open yourself to a possible synchronicity—that is, a meaningful coincidence—by asking the universe or your unconscious for advice or by taking a divinatory walk from time to time and simply noticing what happens along the way. As a result, you'll allow your inner knowing to direct a piece of your life's trajectory.

Also, you might find that an oracle responds not to your stated question, but to a more important issue that's been weighing on your mind. More than once I've set an issue on my mental back burner without ever formulating a question, only to find the answer bubbling up from my unconscious days or weeks later.

then, find your oracle

AFTER DEVISING A QUESTION, you're ready to use *The World Is Your Oracle* to choose a divination method. Here's how: As you pick up the book, let your attention rest lightly on your query. Repeat it—either silently or out loud—as you look for an appropriate oracular method. One of the best ways to begin your search for a technique is to decide first on which intuitive sense—visual, auditory, or kinesthetic—you want to use. (Read more about these different intuitive abilities in the section on "Your Primary Intuitive Sense," p. 21.)

If you don't wish to choose a divination method based on one of the three intuitive senses, you can pick a technique that simply appeals to you most in that moment or seems best for the question, the time and place, and the materials you have on hand. (As you become more familiar with *The World Is Your Oracle*, you can explore other ways to choose a divination method. Several of them are discussed in "Other Ways to Select Divinations," p. 25.)

now, prepare your space

ONCE YOU'VE SELECTED the divination method, read through the directions and assemble everything you'll need. Then, acknowledge the technique you've chosen as a source of wisdom. You might even want to affirm this out loud. Linking with your oracle at the outset of the divination creates a personal bond—both with your means of gaining guidance and with the wisdom that emerges.

From time to time, you might feel the need to begin a divination by purifying the place where you perform it. On those occasions, it's also a good idea to create sacred space, ask for guidance, and set your intentions. And with or without these steps, it's important to always ground and center. Here are some techniques you might use to prepare the space in which your divination will take place.

PURIFY. Cleansing the area in which you'll undertake the oracle clears it of anything that might interfere with the divination, a practice that is particularly important when you have a major stake in the outcome of a divination. Burn a smudge stick, shake a rattle, sprinkle the area with water, or sweep it with a broom in order to let go of any unconscious hopes or conscious aspirations for a specific answer. This will also clear away negative feelings about the situation that has led you to perform a divination, feelings that might otherwise block your inner wisdom. The act of purifying the space allows you to metaphorically clear your mind as well.

CREATE SACRED SPACE. On the occasions when you purify before a divination, you should also create sacred space—a place where you can shake off your day-to-day thoughts and activities and invite a glimpse of mystery into your experience. There are several ways to do this, and they all involve separating the designated oracular space from the everyday. For example, stand in the middle of your space and, as your eyes scan its periphery, imagine that it is encircled by white light or a line of blue flames. Or, walk along its border, carrying a pair of scissors or a knife to cut or "carve out" a space apart. Alternatively, you could create a literal boundary for your space, enclosing the spot with rocks or sticks— or you could blow bubbles as you walk around its margins. Ultimately, though, the action by which you mark this sacred place is less important than your intent in creating it. Stepping outside your everyday space allows you to move beyond your routine mind-set and to embrace the new ideas that come to you.

ASK FOR GUIDANCE AND SET YOUR INTENTIONS. If you create sacred space, then it's important to call upon any teachers, guides, Gods, Goddesses, elementals, plant or animal spirits, or others whom you believe would be willing to help you during your divination. For some people, this may be an unnecessary step; for me, it's sometimes essential. Once you have invited your helpers, add a variation of the golden rule: Ask that your divination serve only the highest and deepest good for all concerned. (When life has gotten messy, I find that it's especially important to include this ethical injunction.) By activating a magical space, these preparations invite experiences that are vibrant and full of synchronicity—and, ultimately, a more fulfilling divination.

GROUND AND CENTER. Whether you've purified and created sacred space or not, it's important that you begin every oracle with a grounding and centering practice. This step will gently nudge you into the present moment, and it'll also take the edge off any tension, like anxiety, excitement, or the strain that comes from trying too hard. All of these things have a tendency to block oracular counsel.

Mindfulness meditation offers the best-known technique for grounding and centering. It shifts you out of your normal, everyday consciousness into a calmer, more relaxed state. Plus, when you meditate, alpha waves increase in your brain, readying you, as scientists have recently shown, for an "aha" moment or an oracular insight (see chapter 2).

Practicing mindfulness meditation isn't difficult. You simply follow your breath. Here's how:

1. Find a quiet place where you won't be interrupted.

2. Sit comfortably. If seated in a chair, place your feet about shoulder-width apart and lengthen your spine in a relaxed way.

3. Gently follow your breath for three to five minutes by thinking to yourself, "I am breathing in," as you inhale, and "I am breathing out," as you exhale.

meditation is a great way to ground and center, but you can use many other techniques. for instance, you could

- **light a candle;**
- **burn incense;**
- **play quiet instrumental music to help you settle down; or**
- **request mental clarity from one of your guides.**

When you're grounded and centered, you'll feel relaxed. Your breathing will slow. Your muscles will feel loose and limp. You might even feel heavier, since you'll notice the weight of your body as you sit in your chair or on the floor. It might also feel as if time has slowed down, and you'll move into a state of stillness, quiet, and calm.

This state is also known as *trance*, a condition of inward reflection. In this semiconscious state, you respond less to external stimuli than you would in a normal waking state. But your unconscious mind, with its intuitions and insights, becomes more accessible to you. During some of the divination techniques in this book, you will move from the light trance established by grounding and centering to a somewhat deeper trance. This state is more like sleep, during which you become less aware of your surroundings and even more open to your unconscious mind.

Once you're grounded and centered, you're ready to undertake your divination.

experience the divination

WHEN ALL THE PRELIMINARIES are done, the divination process begins. That's when you connect with your inner knowing. This is highly individual: For me, it is the spark of the divine within me, but for others, it may represent their higher or deeper selves, an ancestor, or simply the accumulated wisdom of their years. However you choose to envision it, your inner knowing is the part of you that has a greater depth of insight than your ordinary ego-based persona.

In order to awaken your intuition, you need to let go of any desired outcome. And you also need to warmly anticipate an answer to your oracular question. Science has now shown that this attitude is the best for divination: A warm, positive mood makes us more expansive in our expectations for a successful oracle.[A] So smile as you begin your oracle, since science has shown that the very act of smiling produces a happier mood.

Even though the divination you've selected has been devised to use a particular sense (visual, auditory, or kinesthetic), you may see an image, hear a voice, or feel guidance arising in some other form. If so, it's important to accept this as part of your oracle. Remember that divination has its own pathways as well as its own timetable. So please use my time suggestions in the various oracles as guidelines, not rules. Sometimes your understanding will come during your oracle or immediately afterward. Sometimes it will arrive days, or even weeks, later.

interpret the results

ORACLES' GUIDANCE OFTEN COMES in images, symbols, and metaphors, which may be enigmatic, poetic, or dreamlike, rather than clear, direct, or succinct. When your oracle isn't immediately clear, you need to allow the symbols, words, or experiences to "speak" to you as you mull them over in your mind. Free association furnishes the best tool for this process.

USE FREE ASSOCIATION. This technique allows you to approach the meaning of a divination from a number of directions and to draw out your personal associations with its images, words, symbols, or other oracular outcomes. Through this process, you will come closer and closer to understanding its message, until eventually you'll know what it means.

Here's how to do it. Let's assume that you've uncovered an image in your divination that you can't figure out. To interpret its meaning, pose one of the following questions to freely associate with it. Simply ask this question over and over again until you hit upon an answer that rings true for you. Choose the question that works best for you:

- What associations do you have with the image?

- How does this image relate to you?

- What links does this image have to your oracular question?

- What does the image mean to you?

- What feelings does the image evoke in you?

- What is the image trying to tell you?

You'll know that you've discovered the meaning of your oracle when the answer resonates for you. Some people will experience this resonance as an "aha," some as a visual "yes," and others as a feeling that the answer simply "clicks." In any case, you will know when you've understood your oracular image. Just trust your intuition, and the meaning will become clear.

BUILD YOUR OWN SYMBOLIC VOCABULARY. I rarely recommend books of symbols to beginning diviners. In the long run, you'll benefit more from developing your own vocabulary of oracular images, a language that will grow in significance with each oracle you perform. This holds true for many types of divination, including dreams, painting or drawing oracles, and any other type of oracle that leads to a symbolic interpretation. It's also the reason I've left an open space for your personal meanings in all tables of common associations in the sections about **Body Sense, Creatures,** and **Numbers**. The dream group in which I participated for over twelve years had only one rule: The dreamer knows. By this we meant that only the dreamer could interpret the symbols in his or her own dream, because, although we share a common culture, we've had very different individual experiences.

For example, the stereotypical image of a witch is an evil old woman who casts spells on others for her own wicked ends. But "witch" may call other things to mind, too, like a neighborhood child dressed up for trick-or-treat; the smartest girl in the class at a fictional school for wizards; or a modern-day practitioner of Wicca (an earth-centered, mystical tradition that recognizes all of nature as sacred).

Give yourself time to find your own meanings for the images you encounter. Remember, though, that building your symbolic vocabulary takes time. When some people begin to engage in divinations, they jump in headfirst. They start to see their entire world as symbolic. If you find yourself overinterpreting every little thing in your life in this way, use your common sense to temper this tendency. As Freud may have said years ago, "Sometimes a cigar is just a cigar!"

WAIT TO HEAR AN ANSWER. Occasionally, the answer to an oracular question may elude you. There are several possible reasons for this. The pieces of your divinatory puzzle may still be coming together. You may not yet be ready to face the answer to your oracle. Or, this may not be the right time for an answer for some other reason. And sometimes you may encounter resistance within yourself, because you really don't want to hear the answer you'll uncover.

Even if it takes some time to arrive, an answer can be well worth the wait. I believe that we constantly receive information from our unconscious minds about the quandaries in our lives, guidance that can steer our decisions in positive directions. After all, any type of divination or psychic reading ultimately affirms what we already know on some level. With practice, we can learn how to access this counsel when we need it. It's just a matter of discovering how to attune ourselves to our deeper truth in order to retrieve our intuitive knowledge.[5]

Especially in these hectic, confusing times, oracles allow us to discover our own motivations, feelings, and thoughts about our questions, and can help us to become aware of the paths our lives are taking. Divination offers clues about where we're headed, affirmations that we're on the right track, or indications that it's time to take a detour. In short, divination gives us the tools to chart our own courses or to become our own life coaches.

finally, honor your divination

GIVE THANKS. When you've interpreted your latest oracle and gleaned the insights it has to offer, it's a good idea to express your gratitude for its guidance. In fact, I think it's important to admit your debt to the powers that helped you perform an oracle with their encouragement, inspiration, and advice. Conveying gratitude also allows you to acknowledge the beauty and truth of the universe you've seen reflected in your oracle. Since I believe that divination links us with the sacred, I naturally respond with a sense of reverence and gratitude. I treasure those moments when I feel my life aligned with the holy.

RECORD WHAT YOU'VE LEARNED. When you've finished interpreting your divination, record it in an oracle journal. These written accounts are valuable. They will provide you with a history of your personal growth and the decisions that led to it. And when your life seems lackluster, rereading your divinatory log will also remind you of the magic that happens when you touch the realm of wisdom and insight that oracles open to you.

RESPOND CREATIVELY. Occasionally, you might want to celebrate your divinations by creating art inspired by them. Such creative activity can take many forms: masks, drawings, collages, stories, poetry, ritual objects, rituals themselves, dramas, comic strips, or songs, to name just a few. Whichever form you choose, know that, in fashioning art from your oracles, you're following a long tradition of divinatory enacting and fabricating. In fact, much indigenous art derives from oracular experiences: Inuit spirit masks, Aboriginal bark paintings of Dreamtime figures, and Huichol yarn drawings are all derived from shamanic visions. If you create such an "object of inner wisdom," leave it someplace where you'll see it often in your daily life in order to remind yourself of your oracle and the wisdom it offered you.

your primary intuitive sense

CONTEMPORARY RESEARCH IN "embodied cognition" describes how we use our senses in order to think. In my divination workshops, I've learned that we not only think with our senses, we also employ them in divination. And I've come to appreciate that some people are more alert to oracles that emphasize sight (visual diviners), some have an easier time with divinations that use sound (auditory diviners), while still others draw on sensation or movement to unlock their inner knowing (kinesthetic diviners). That's why the oracular methods in this book are classified under these three categories.

One of the most valuable approaches to take with *The World Is Your Oracle* involves performing divinations that employ what I call your primary intuitive sense. This is the sense—visual, auditory, or kinesthetic—that most effectively relays information from your unconscious mind to your conscious awareness.

SECOND SIGHT, INNER VOICE, AND GUT FEELINGS

Visual divination is often referred to as "second sight." The people who use this oracular sense are the least common within the population of North America. Those with "second sight" tend to see images, colors, shapes, or other types of symbols when they perform divinations. Some of the people who are most adept at visual oracles even view mini-movies in their heads. All of these oracles may come through either the physical eyes or the inner eyes, also known as the "mind's eye."

Auditory diviners receive oracular information through words, noises, and music, by listening either to their "inner voice" or to external sounds. Musicians and other people sensitive to sound are often auditory diviners. As someone who prefers auditory oracles, I often hear familiar tunes in my head. The words to these songs contain messages for me if I stop to think about them.

Kinesthetic diviners may be the most numerous group in North America today. They include people who are empaths and those who listen to their own "vibes." Empathy involves a close reading of other people's emotions, while "vibes" or gut feelings are physical sensations that give insight into particular situations or individuals. I believe that most of us have at least an embryonic kinesthetic sense that can be developed with practice.

ARE YOU VISUAL, AUDITORY, OR KINESTHETIC?

You can often figure out which of these senses works best for your oracles by simply answering the question, "Are you auditory, visual, or kinesthetic?" But if you're not sure, you can also use the following meditative techniques to gauge your sensory tendencies. These one-to-two-minute exercises will indicate which sense is your primary intuitive sense. Try each of them and make a note to yourself about which one(s) works best to ground and center you:

A. Close your eyes. Then feel your breath as it moves in and out of your nostrils. Let this sensation take you deeply into the stillness beneath it. Feel and listen deeply for a minute or two.

B. Close your eyes. Then listen to the ambient noise in your environment, like the wind in the trees, children playing in the street, or the air conditioner humming in the background. Use the sounds you hear to sink deeply into the calm feelings beneath them. Listen and feel deeply for a minute or two.

C. Turn on some quiet music or white noise, like the noise of a rattle or the hiss between two FM radio stations. Then feel your breath as it moves in and out of your nostrils. Let this sensation take you deeply into the darkness or color beneath it. Feel and look deeply for a minute or two.

D. Turn on some quiet music or white noise, as above. Then stare at a mandala or a photo of natural beauty. Let this vision take you into the calm feelings beneath it. Look and feel deeply for a minute or two.

E. Rock calmly back and forth or walk around the room. While continuing to rock or walk, listen to the ambient noise in your environment, as above. Use the sounds you hear to sink deeply into the darkness or color beneath them. Listen and look deeply for a minute or two.

F.   Rock calmly back and forth or walk around the room. While continuing to rock or walk, stare at a mandala or a photo of natural beauty. Let this vision take you into the stillness beneath it. Look and listen deeply for a minute or two.

Now look back on your experience and ask yourself these questions about each technique:

- Did you feel grounded and centered?

- Was the experience easy and comfortable?

- Which sense quieted down as you grounded and centered: the visual, auditory, or kinesthetic?

If you have answered "yes" to the first two questions for a particular grounding and centering exercise, the final question often tells you which sense is your primary intuitive sense. You can also look at which techniques grounded and centered you best. If A or C worked best for you, that indicates that you're a **kinesthetic** diviner. If B or E worked best for you, you're probably an **auditory** diviner. And if D or F worked best, you're probably a **visual** diviner.

Now, in order to confirm your primary intuitive sense, try one of the simpler divination techniques that employ that sense. Try the **Body Sense** oracle if you think you're kinesthetic; the **Guided Meditation** divination if you believe you're auditory; or the **Ashes** divination if you suspect you're visual. At the end of this chapter, I've listed each divination method under the sensory category to which it belongs—auditory, visual, or kinesthetic—so that you can easily identify those divination methods you may wish to use.

If you've practiced a traditional form of divination for some time, knowing your primary intuitive sense will also enhance your experience. Traditional systems like tarot cards, runes, or the *I Ching* usually depend on guidance couched in words (usually sentences or phrases) or advice based on an interlocking set of symbols. The visual, auditory, and kinesthetic senses are your means of recognizing the symbols or words of these time-honored divinations. By working with your primary oracular sense, you can build your intuitive skills and develop a deeper understanding of the symbols and techniques you've been using for years.

Knowing your primary intuitive sense will also help you interpret your oracle. If you're a visual diviner, you can unfocus your mind's eye and allow thoughts and images to arise as you ask yourself what your divination means until one idea finally nudges you into understanding. If auditory oracles work best for you, you may hear the meaning of your oracle in words, music, or sounds. And if kinesthetic divinations provide guidance for you, your interpretation may arrive as a feeling.

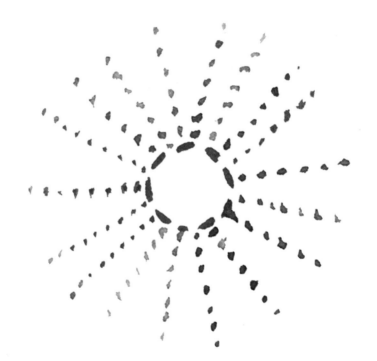

other ways to select divinations

BEYOND USING YOUR primary intuitive sense, there are a number of other ways that you can organize your use of the oracular techniques in this book.

BASIC AND ADVANCED ORACLES

Each entry in chapters 3 to 5 is marked with a label indicating that it's either a basic, straightforward divination method or a more advanced, open-ended technique, which demands more experience with your intuitive skills. To help you get started with the basic oracles, I've compiled lists of common associations with **Body Sense, Creatures,** and **Numbers**. You'll find them at the end of each of these divination entries. These lists should help you understand possible correlations between your oracular outcome and its likely meaning. Of course, it's important to remember that if you have personal associations with any of the symbols I've listed, you'll usually find them more meaningful than those that appear on my lists.

After undertaking the basic oracles, you can work your way through more advanced divination methods. **Meditation** is a good example of an advanced practice, since it's a technique that incorporates a period of meditating followed by a silent time during which you may gain insight into your question. If you already have a strongly developed intuitive sense, you might gravitate toward the more advanced oracles like **Scrying** or listening to your **Intuition** rather than those with more basic, straightforward results.

ASTROLOGY

Earth, Air, Fire, and **Water** make up four of the divination methods I've collected in this book. If you know your astrological sun sign, you can begin with the element that rules that sign. If earth signs predominate in your birth chart, divination methods that link you with your body—or with the physical in some other way—will be most useful: **Body Sense, Clay, Dance, Dowsing, Hands and Feet, Mudras,** and **Walking** are the first you can try. If, however, air governs your chart, you should look for cognitive types of oracles—like **Books, Mind Maps, Repeated Cues,** or **Journaling**—since air corresponds to mental or intellectual pursuits. For those of you with "fiery" astrological personalities, take a look at the section titled **Fire** to get started—or begin with any technique with which you sense a passionate connection. And for those of you who feel most at ease in the emotional depths of life—because water governs your horoscope—the method listed under **Water** offers a likely candidate, as well as any oracle with which you feel an immediate emotional rapport.

CYCLE THROUGH THE ORACLES

Since this book contains forty methods in total, another approach would be to check out one of them each week until you've covered all techniques. This approach has its advantages: Using all the methods in this way will provide you with an overview of the divinatory practices included here. I also recommend performing divinations on your birthday, at the beginning of the year, on anniversaries, or on other significant dates. Such oracles often yield greater insight, since these dates hold special meaning for you.

FOLLOW A THEME

Using this book thematically offers another possible method for exploring its depths. For instance, if your query has to do with family matters, contact one of your **Ancestors**, since deceased relatives tend to have a good overview of familial situations. If your question brings up a topic that can be answered with a simple yes or no, **Dowsing** will serve you well. If your issue concerns illness or injury, a kinesthetic oracle is appropriate, since divinations like **Body Sense** or **Hands and Feet** relate to the body and its sensations. And if your query concerns an area in your life that reminds you of the physical **(Earth)**, the mental **(Air)**, the emotional **(Water)**, or willpower and passion **(Fire)**, employing a divination that corresponds to that particular element will help you get in touch with your inner knowing (see "Astrology," p. 25).

COMBINED ORACLES

Once you're familiar with the variety of divination methods in this book, you can combine different types to seek a more multifaceted answer. One way to do this would be to use one of your favorite **Books** to search for the first **Creature** you come across. You could also notice the **Number** of **People** you encounter while performing a divinatory **Walk**. Or, you could use **Sculpting Your Insight** to answer the first part of your oracular question and a **Chanting** divination to answer the second half. Just be careful when you combine oracular methods to avoid controlling the outcome of your divination. Remember that attempts at manipulating your divination will weaken its effectiveness.

use your intuition

IF YOU FIND THAT varying your means of divination keeps your life vibrant and your connection with spirit open and fluid, by all means use different types of divinations. But if, after using the oracles gathered in this book, you discover that one or two methods work best for you, I encourage you to focus your future divinations on those techniques. In either case, *The World Is Your Oracle* will have served its purpose. Your life will be enriched by regular oracular readings that put you in touch with the web of life of which you are a part.

Enjoy your explorations of the many oracular techniques gathered here. As you'll see in the next chapter, they provide scientifically proven methods of awakening your intuition—and the results can feel both thrilling and enlightening.

techniques categorized by sense

VISUAL TECHNIQUES

ORACLE	TECHNIQUE NAME	TECHNIQUE DESCRIPTION
Air	Winds of Change	This modern form of wind divination (*austromancy*) allows you to read your oracle in the movements of an object blown by the wind.
*Ashes	A Burning Answer to Your Question	Watching a piece of paper transform into ash facilitates your oracular insight.
*Balloon Diagrams	Mapping Your Mind's Genius	Creating a visual map of your issue will shed new light on it.
*Books	A Fortuitous Word	Open a book at random, point your finger at one of the pages, and read what's written there.
Candles	Light Illumines the Water	Relax in a warm bath and let the candlelight reflecting off the water mesmerize you into a calm state of mind with greater access to your inner knowing.
*Creatures	Guidance from the Wild	Walk through a favorite park or natural area with a question in mind and notice which creature(s) you see.

ORACLE	TECHNIQUE NAME	TECHNIQUE DESCRIPTION
Dreams	Awakening to Insight	Prime yourself to dream about your oracular question and awaken to insight.
Mirrors	Reflecting Your Feelings	Intuit new perspectives about your issue by noticing the play of your facial expressions in a mirror.
*Numbers	Numerical Wisdom	Create a deck of number cards, then choose one as your divination.
Scrying	Gazing into Your Inner Well	Stare at water with a soft focus for five to ten minutes or until an answer to your question surfaces.
Spirit Guides	Inner Journey for Guidance	Enter the wisdom of the spirit world by following the lead of your spirit guide.
Stars	Cosmic Connect-the-Dots	After going outside at night, notice which quadrant of the sky calls to you and what image(s) you see there.

*Indicates basic technique. All others are more advanced.

AUDITORY TECHNIQUES

ORACLE	TECHNIQUE NAME	TECHNIQUE DESCRIPTION
Ancestors	Contacting an Elder	Encourage a deceased loved one to offer you guidance about an issue.
Birds	Avian Advice	Listen to the warbling, squeals, trills, and melodies of the birds around you and note what their song suggests to you.
Chanting	Singing the Mystery Awake	Slip into an altered state of mind while singing a familiar hymn or song.
*Divine Inspiration	Dialogue with the Sacred	Address whatever deity or aspect of the sacred that you feel will best answer your query.
Drumming	The Steady Pulse of Spirit	A steady beat on the drum pulls the scattered pieces of your mind into a vibrant state that's open to your inner guidance.
Fire	Whispers of Flame	The hiss and crackle of a fire produce sounds within which you hear your oracular insight.
*Guided Meditation	Your Wise Friend's Counsel	Imagine walking through a beautiful landscape to meet a wise being who tells you what you need to know.

ORACLE	TECHNIQUE NAME	TECHNIQUE DESCRIPTION
Intuition	Listening with Inner Ears	Imagine that your ear canals extend into the vital energy (*qi*) at the center of your body in order to tune into your intuition.
Leaves	Rustling Messages	Within the rustles, scratches, creaks, and rasps of the leaves on your chosen tree or bush, you listen to the voice of your inner wisdom.
*People	A Stranger Gives You Direction	In a public place, ask your question silently or under your breath and then wait for a stranger to answer it.
*Repeated Cues	Brainstorming New Perspectives	Responding to repeated cues, you hear yourself uttering new insights about your issue.
*Sounds	Echoes of Your Spirit	Ask your question out loud and then listen for a sound(s) that gives you an answer.
Toning	Sounds from Your Depths	Intuit and create the sounds or noises that will lead to greater understanding of your divination question.
Water	Ripples of Truth	The sound of an ocean, stream, or lake will float information forward in your mind.

*Indicates basic technique. All others are more advanced.

KINESTHETIC TECHNIQUES

ORACLE	TECHNIQUE NAME	TECHNIQUE DESCRIPTION
*Body Sense	Getting in Touch	Follow a guided meditation to tap into your body's wisdom.
*Clay	Sculpting Your Insight	Work clay with your eyes closed until you create a piece to interpret as your oracle.
Dance	Ecstatic Enlightenment	Dance until you're euphoric and then channel the energy raised to your spiritual core, letting it rest gently on your question.
*Dowsing	Divining with Fingers and Thumbs	Press the thumb and pinkie of your nondominant hand together and try to break the contact with your dominant index finger to answer an either/or question.
Earth	Hands-On Wisdom	As you feel the weight and texture of a large rock in your hands, let your mind drift to your question and see what surfaces for you.
Hands and Feet	Your Body's Signals	Notice where your feet want to take you or what your hands want to do as a pathway to greater insight into your issue.
*Journaling	Third-Page Divination	Using an adapted version of Julia Cameron's "morning pages," tap into your creative flow and find new ways of approaching your issue.

ORACLE	TECHNIQUE NAME	TECHNIQUE DESCRIPTION
Meditation	Mindful Knowing	Calmly follow your breath as it deepens and slows, allowing your mind to find greater clarity about your issue.
Mudras	Touching Spirit with Finger Yoga	Assume a traditional hand position to facilitate your understanding of a situation in your life.
*Painting and Drawing	Creativity Unleashed	Let your hand move across the paper in whatever way feels best and then interpret what you've drawn as your oracle.
Sacred Sites	Connecting to Source	Open yourself to the wisdom of the sacred site you have chosen.
Smudging	Burning Confusion Away	As smoke washes over your body, all unnecessary thoughts, sensations, and feelings blow away, so you can attend to your issue without their interference.
Trees	Taproot to Within	While hugging or touching a favorite tree, sense the answer to your question.
Walking	Zen Concentration Walk	While thinking about your question as if it were a *koan*, walk mindfully to experience your reality as it truly is.

*Indicates basic technique. All others are more advanced.

2

SCIENCE
AND
DIVINATION

S CIENCE IS FINALLY CATCHING UP with the wisdom traditions of the world. With breakthroughs in technology, research has begun to shed light on how divination acts to facilitate "aha moments," those creative insights that seem to come to us spontaneously. In the last ten to fifteen years, studies have shown that flashes of insight occur when a person's brain is in a particular state. This is exactly the frame of mind that seers and sages have known about for millennia, a mind-set you can promote by taking a leisurely walk in the woods, letting your mind wander, or by performing a divination. In this altered state, science has now shown, new ideas often pop into your awareness. This chapter will explain how the brain creates this mental state and suggests scientifically proven methods to improve your oracular practice—insights that will clarify why the little rituals in chapter 1 set the stage for a successful divination.

THE "BRAIN BLINK"

Neuroscientists have discovered that every piece of information stored in the brain has associations with other thoughts, so that each thought calls to mind the next idea and so on, until you have a "stream of consciousness." Some of these associations are remote and, as a result, are unlikely to come to mind, while many are almost automatic. Our conscious, analytical minds remain wedded to the most obvious associations we have—those that stem from our experiences, what we read in books and other media, and our assumptions about the world. Most of the time, the "mental box" created by these seemingly self-evident associations allows us to anticipate and understand our lives rapidly. But these habitual associations also limit our thinking, sometimes causing a one-track mind.[A] This can be detrimental when we're presented with new challenges in our lives. So, when we're stuck in this way of thinking, we need an aha moment or a divination to free our thoughts. Then our minds can associate with the more remote ideas found in the unconscious, allowing new perceptions to surface into our conscious awareness.

The most recent research[A] demonstrates that aha moments happen when two conditions are met. First, there's a burst of alpha brain wave activity called a "brain blink." This sudden increase of alpha waves diverts awareness from a person's surroundings. The result is "the power to ignore," or what scientists call "optimal inattention,"[6] reducing distractions so the mind can become aware of less obvious unconscious thoughts, also called remote associations. It's very like a situation in which someone asks you a difficult question and you look away in order to give your undivided attention to your answer: Glancing to one side redirects you away from extraneous factors, like your interrogator's facial expressions. And your brain does the same thing. When you're asked something challenging, an answer might already be activated at an unconscious level. But there's always a lot of noise and distraction blocking it, so you can't retrieve it without a "brain blink." Thanks to this neural diversion, novel ideas bubble up from the unconscious into awareness.

If we survey divination techniques, we find that they operate in a similar way. The state in which divination takes place—sometimes meditative, sometimes euphoric, sometimes characterized by "brain wave entrainment"[7]—is in each case distinguished by alpha waves in the occipital lobe of the brain, exactly where the "brain blink" takes place. What's more, the very techniques of inward focus fostered by divination are designed to suppress or ignore unnecessary sensations; that is, to create "optimal inattention."

The wisdom keepers of the world realized this long ago. They knew that in order to let go of their narrow, habitual responses to the situations and people around them—as well as the questions they faced—they had to take a walk in the woods, meditate, drum, or dance ecstatically. In other words, neuroscientists have discovered what ancient and indigenous seers have always known: that the glare of the external world can block insight.

A BURST OF ACTIVITY IN
THE RIGHT HEMISPHERE

The second mental condition that characterizes an aha moment or a successful divination occurs when a spark of insight flashes from the unconscious mind into consciousness. On EEG and fMRI scans, this burst of neural activity happens in the right temporal lobe of the brain, directly above the right ear. The brain's right hemisphere, where these flashes of insight occur, has been shown to be the major origin for creative thoughts. The reason for this is that it has a much larger number of associations with any concept or problem. In contrast, the left hemisphere is the site of our restricted "mental box," where analytical thinking takes place. When we think analytically about a problem, our mental activity remains focused and exclusive, boxed in by the left hemisphere of the brain. This kind of thinking inhibits our associative, broadly inclusive right hemisphere from making new connections. But with the help of alpha waves and the optimal inattention they create, the brain sets aside the left hemisphere's habitual and restricted thinking so that it can tune into alternate interpretations from the unconscious, accessing what neuroscientists call "insight"[A] and divination experts call an oracle. So how can we tap into this insight?

strategies for successful divination

RESEARCH SHOWS THAT the unconscious works better than the conscious mind in complicated situations, allowing us to integrate complex information in a more holistic way. It's the source of our creativity, our insight, and, of course, the aha moments we've been exploring here.[8] Oracular methods give us access to these powerful faculties. And science has recently demonstrated a number of techniques that can make our divinations even more successful.[A] Here are a few:

- **SMILE.** The very act of smiling has been shown to produce happier moods. And positive emotions like joy, tranquility, or love facilitate aha moments.

- **LET GO OF YOUR WORRIES AND TRUST IN THE OUTCOME OF YOUR ORACLE.** Anxiety leads to analytical thinking and keeps you stuck on the obvious, while trust opens you to greater insight.

- **BROADEN YOUR ATTENTION IN ORDER TO BROADEN YOUR THINKING.** Science has demonstrated that some of the same mental mechanisms that regulate the scope of your vision also regulate the scope of your thinking. You can broaden your attention just by going outside or to a large indoor space like a cathedral. You can also broaden your attention by using peripheral vision; that is, noticing your entire visual field out to its edges, so that your vision (often) appears blurry. When your mental scope expands in response to the breadth of your vision, you begin to reconfigure your thoughts into a new, meaningful whole, a proven practice for inducing flashes of insight.

- **LET YOUR MIND WANDER OR UNFOCUS YOUR ATTENTION IN SOME OTHER WAY.** Science shows us that most creative people tend to daydream a lot.

- **FOCUS INWARD.** You can do this by using any of the preparation suggestions in chapter 1 or through sensory restriction. You can restrict what your senses perceive in a number of ways. For instance, research demonstrates that darkened rooms are effective, because you can't see much in them. Silence or white noise is also good, because you can't hear much beyond it. A shower or warm bath makes it difficult to feel the boundary of your skin, so your sense of touch becomes less acute. (I use all three of these types of sensory restriction in **Candles: Light Illumines the Water.**)

- **INCUBATE YOUR DIVINATION.** Science has now shown that unconscious incubation is what generates insights, since hidden relationships brought from the unconscious to the forefront of the mind are the material from which sudden realizations are drawn. Incubation involves taking time away from your issue or problem: The further away you get, the better. The easiest way to incubate an oracle is by sleeping on your question (see **Dreams**). But you can also take a short break from a problem that has you stumped. Walking in nature works well, especially if it's somewhere you've never been. Doing this will also give you a change of context (see below), so that your mind will have an opportunity to let go of its first thoughts about your issue.

- **USE AN "AHA SYMBOL."** A classic example would be an incandescent lightbulb or a sparkler, but many people have their own emblems for creative insight, including particular animals or crystals. Scientists have shown that simply seeing such symbols enhances sudden insights. So place your "aha symbol"—or a drawing or photograph of it—where you can see it often.

- **CHANGE YOUR CONTEXT.** You can do this by going to a new place, or you can think about the life of an unusual or unusually creative person and travel imaginatively in his or her shoes. Either of these activities will prime you to be more creative.

- **PERFORM YOUR DIVINATION AT THE LOW POINT OF YOUR DAY.** Peak productivity and peak performance coincide with the high point of your analytical thinking. If you're a night owl, perform your divination in the morning. If you're an early bird, do it in the evening.

how ritual prepares you for a "brain blink"

NOW YOU KNOW HOW TO set the stage for an insight-inducing "brain blink"—but, from a scientific perspective, why do these strategies work? When you reach out to divination for answers, you're often feeling frustrated, upset, or stuck in some way. Research has found that negative emotions, especially anxiety, reinforce analytical thinking and inhibit flashes of insight. In fact, being overly concerned about something can lead to "tunnel vision," which you want to avoid. The little rituals I suggested in chapter 1 (**Purify, Create Sacred Space, Ask for Guidance and Set Your Intentions**, as well as **Grounding and Centering**, p. 14) will counteract these mental states, since their purpose is in part to induce a positive mood—which, scientific research has shown, will also invite a "brain blink."

BRIGHTEN YOUR SPIRITS

In chapter 1, I discussed how purifying the space in which you undertake a divination can brighten your spirits and help you become more peaceful. The intent of this ceremony is to clear your mind of extraneous thoughts or feelings that might interfere with your oracle. The symbolism of cleansing can sweep away your negative emotions as well as any desires you have for a specific outcome. This is a good thing, since science has shown that positive moods like tranquility, joy, or love increase the likelihood of an aha moment.[A]

LEAVE THE HABITUAL BEHIND

These preliminary rituals can also separate you from your everyday perspective—the normal analytical mind-set that keeps your thinking boxed-in and exclusive. When you **Create Sacred Space** or perform similar ceremonies, you're stepping outside of your everyday routines. Physical actions—such as separating your designated oracular space from the rest of your house by surrounding it with stones—imprint their significance on the body as well as the mind, and, as a result, have a stronger impact than simply contemplating your intention or stating it out loud.

You've probably noticed that thinking is almost always associated with the contexts in which you have thoughts. For example, while upstairs, you remember that you left your smartphone downstairs. But by the time you descend to the living room, you've forgotten what it was you wanted to retrieve. Once upstairs again, you remember that it was your cell phone you were trying to find. Similarly, changing your context by separating yourself from your normal haunts helps you overcome your obvious "first thoughts." This is what scientists call "fixation forgetting."[A] Once you've left your habitual judgments and assessments behind, it's easier to think "outside the box."

SEE THE BIG PICTURE

The preparatory practices in chapter 1 can also broaden your outlook. Calling on the sacred (in some form) to guide your divination enlarges your thinking from your small, personal point of view to include the larger perspective of the divine. Seeing a bigger picture is another scientifically proven practice that induces flashes of insight. It's one of the best ways to notice more of the interconnecting pieces that make up your puzzle—even those that seem unimportant.[A]

GROUNDING AND CENTERING

Grounding and centering can bring about all of these changes, which is why it's so important to meditate or ground and center in some other way before you begin your divination. It takes the edge off any negative emotions you bring to your divination, and it also transforms your mind-set from one that's stuck in a pattern of habitual thinking to one that can contain a more spacious form of understanding. Plus, the alpha waves that occur while meditating can create a "brain blink."

From grounding and centering to interpreting an oracle, the divinations in this book fully encompass the two prerequisites for an aha moment and offer a more colorful and varied guidebook for you to follow. While science is just beginning to chart flashes of insight in the brain, people all over the world have been using divination for centuries, if not millennia. These time-honored practices will answer your questions and expand your intuitive skills. In performing oracles, you will discover your motivations, feelings, and thoughts about your questions, becoming more aware of your life's journey. And in connecting with your deepest wisdom, divination will encourage your personal and spiritual growth.

3

VISUAL

TECHNIQUES

V ISUAL ORACLES ARE AMONG the most common in our culture. Think of tarot cards, the *I Ching*, runes, or reading tea leaves. In one sense this seems paradoxical since visual diviners are the least prevalent in our population. But the fact is that our society is extremely visual and is becoming even more so, given the popularity of smartphones, tablets, and personal computers.

The visual divinations gathered here run the gamut from simple and straightforward (for example, randomly opening a book and selecting an oracular text with your eyes closed) to highly advanced (like staring into water until an answer surfaces). But all of them depend on identifying images, objects, symbols, or movements— either as insight triggers for your open eyes or through the medium of trance using the mind's eye.

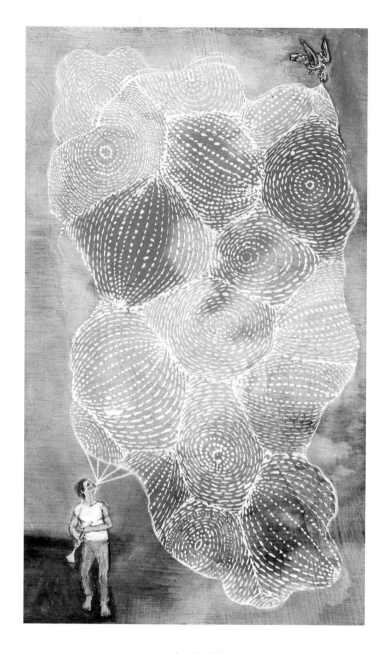

AIR
WINDS OF CHANGE

› ADVANCED ‹

We in the West inherited the Aristotelian view of the elements. Like earlier Greek philosophers, Aristotle believed that all physical matter consisted of four elements—earth, air, fire, and water—but he also added a fifth element: "ether," a heavenly substance from which the stars were born. Theories such as Aristotle's probably had roots in even older traditions in China and India. The Taoists in China referred to five elements—earth, fire, water, metal, and wood—while ancient Hindus in India developed a five-element system that included earth, air, fire, water, and space.

These ideas of the cosmos deeply influenced Western culture until the sixteenth or seventeenth century, when more scientific concepts began to displace them. Fortunately for us, though, Western esotericism preserved these ancient views, keeping them alive in tarot, alchemy, astrology, and even in the four suits found in the common playing cards we still use today.

This heritage also lives on in the personal qualities we associate with the four elements. We describe some people as "fiery," aligning fire with passion and

winds of change:
this modern form of wind
divination (austromancy) allows you
to read your oracle in the movements
of an object blown by the wind.

WHERE — A natural area

WHEN — Daylight

HOW — Sitting or standing

TOOLS — A park, backyard, or wilderness
area where you feel comfortable

A natural object(s) you can
follow with your eyes

short tempers. We view others who seem solid and grounded as "earthy." We link water to people whose emotions flow freely, especially ones that bring tears to the eyes—like joy, frustration, and sorrow. And since we relate the element of air to the mind, an "airy" person may exhibit occasional spaciness as well as visionary tendencies.

These days, air remains an elusive element for most of us. We can't see it, smell it, or taste it—yet we can't live without it. A person will die within minutes if deprived of this life-giving substance. Air's mystery and its necessity to life allow it to behave as an oracle in many ways.

Austromancy provided the ancients with an oracular method that studied the winds. My contemporary form of wind divination allows you to identify the movements of the air by watching it shift a natural object(s) from place to place. As I mentioned in chapter 2, neuroscience has now shown that when you perform a divination like this one outside, both your vision and your thinking will expand, allowing you to tap into your unconscious for new ideas.[A] This oracle works best for people who are visually adept and prefer more advanced oracles.

STEPS

1. Find a natural area (park, woodland, beach, backyard, garden, or wilderness) where you want to perform your divination.

2. Acknowledge this place as your source of guidance.

3. Determine which object(s) will mark the passage of the wind for you, such as a fallen leaf, a tree branch, nearby grasses, or the surface of a pond.

4. Formulate your question (p. 12).

5. Ground and center (p. 15). Let your meditation create a space separate from your everyday life and a mind-set free of your ordinary, analytical thinking.

6. State your question out loud.

7. Watch as the air moves whatever substance you've chosen as your oracle. Let its motion calm you into a deeper and deeper state of relaxation.

8. Continue to notice the movement of your chosen object as the wind tosses it, blows it around, undulates its surface, or plays with it in another way.

9. After a minute or so, begin to observe the wind with your peripheral vision. Look at a spot in the middle distance and allow your awareness to widen until it takes in everything, right out to the edges of your visual field, while still continuing to notice your wind-tossed object. You will soon feel yourself enter a light trance (see chapter 1, p. 16).

10. Remain in this state for five minutes while observing the wind.

11. If after five minutes you haven't received an oracular insight,

restate your question and meditate silently with your eyes closed for five more minutes.

12. Describe for yourself what you've noticed. Interpret the movements you've observed as your oracle. What do these movements remind you of? Are the movements of your object erratic, suggesting something unusual or irregular? Or are they slow and calm, possibly indicating an easy resolution or a long wait? Does the object move in circles? In a straight line? Up and down? Any of these movements could give you oracular information. If your oracle's meaning resists analysis, use free association (p. 18) to unlock its secrets.

13. Thank the air for your oracle.

CONTINUING THE JOURNEY

When doing a visual divination like **Air**, it's always a good idea to use peripheral vision; that is, broadening your awareness until it takes in everything in your visual field. Peripheral vision automatically relaxes your body and quiets your mind. And in this state of heightened alpha waves, it's much more likely that you will receive intuitive wisdom since alpha waves have been shown to be the scientific hallmark for creative insight.[A]

Once in a while, you may notice the movements of the air through the sounds it makes. If so, does the wind whisper an answer to your question? Do any of its sounds remind you of an experience or a thought? (See **Sounds**, p. 147, for interpretive ideas. Or if you've heard a bird call, see **Birds**, p. 235. Or if it's rustling leaves, see **Leaves**, p. 134.) Remember that divination seems to have its own method of conveying oracular information and its own timetable. Insight may arrive while you're engaged in your oracle; after several hours; or sometimes even days later. Try to be patient, and know that a new insight into your issue will come: You might even experience it as a subtle shift in your situation.

ASHES

A BURNING ANSWER TO YOUR QUESTION

› BASIC ‹

Ashes serve as an important symbol in many of the world's religions, so it's no surprise that people also use them in divination. The ancients undertook ash oracles in a variety of forms: *tephramancy* (burning tree bark and then reading the ashes for an answer); *spodomancy* (divining from the behavior and shapes created by cinders or soot); and *libanomancy* (watching how burning incense turns to ash). Most *spodomancy* was performed by writing a question in ash and then noticing how the wind changed the words to spell out an answer: The Greek playwright Aeschylus recorded such a practice utilizing the ashes from a fireplace.[9] In contrast, an adept among the ancient Celts could divine simply by sleeping next to the ashes of an animal burnt as a sacrifice.[10]

Ash oracles still exist in a number of places today. In Mongolia, for instance, a monk layers ash onto a bone from the the shoulder blade of an ox, cow, or sheep. He then reads the oracle in the patterns found on different parts of the bone, each of which corresponds to a particular area in a person's life.[11] In Romani (Gypsy) divination, the seer tosses ashes into the air. She then interprets them based on how evenly they land on the floor: Uniform ashes indicate a positive outcome, while a pile(s) signifies bad fortune.[12] American Indians from several tribes also use ash divination: When a birth or death occurs, the shaman gazes at

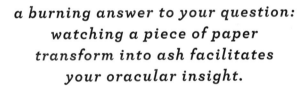

a burning answer to your question:
watching a piece of paper
transform into ash facilitates
your oracular insight.

WHERE — **Near a fire**

WHEN — **Anytime**

HOW — **Sitting or standing**

TOOLS — **A fire**
A piece of paper

the ashes in an extinguished fire the next morning in order to determine the fate of the person after his or her transition.[13]

This technique may prove particularly effective for visual diviners. Seeing the paper on which you've written your query transform into ash provides a powerful visual representation of the change of perspective an oracle can facilitate.

STEPS

1. Prepare a safe place for burning. Collect your tools.

2. Formulate your question (p. 12).

3. Write your question on a small piece of paper.

4. Ground and center (p. 15). Let your meditation create a space separate from your everyday life and a mind-set free of your ordinary, analytical thinking.

5. Start your fire, and when it's burning well, drop your query into the flames.

6. Watch as your question goes up in smoke. Be aware that the smoke itself may provide illumination. Your answer may come at any time during this process and in any form.

7. Once the paper has burned, examine the form(s) taken by the remaining ash (without touching it) for guidance about your question. What pattern(s) do you recognize in this image(s)? How has the flame dispersed the ashes? Is it still one piece or several? What do these signs tell you about your divination?

8. Explore what this shape(s) embodies for you. If your oracle's meaning resists analysis, use free association (p. 18) to unlock its secret.

9. Thank the ash(es) for your oracle.

CONTINUING THE JOURNEY

Safety is important here, so it's best to undertake this oracle outdoors, using a metal bowl or washbasin. Such a container allows you to easily identify the ash created by burning your oracular piece of paper without having to distinguish it from other cinders in a fireplace or campfire.

Sometimes the paper becomes a single large cinder. Be careful not to touch it until you have looked for images, since the ash may disintegrate when you handle it. (Plus, you might burn yourself.) What shape(s) or form(s) do you see in the remains?

If you prefer to burn your query indoors, it's safe to use what I call "Bridget's fire." (Since this fire is contained in a metal bowl resting in water, it uses the two elements associated with the Celtic Goddess Bridget, who eventually became a Catholic saint.) The water absorbs the heat of the blaze without any risk to the surface beneath it, and the fire produces a smokeless flame, making it ideal for indoor use. As you'll see below, once your query has burned, you can clearly distinguish the ash from the remaining Epsom salts.

HOW TO PREPARE BRIDGET'S FIRE

This recipe is for a single piece of paper no larger than a two-inch (5 cm) square. If you plan to burn two or three queries, use proportionately more of each ingredient.

1. Pour 2 tablespoons (28 g) of Epsom salts and 2 tablespoons (28 ml) of rubbing alcohol into a small metal bowl.

2. Place the small metal bowl inside a larger fireproof bowl filled with water: The water will safely absorb the heat from the blaze.

3. Ignite the fire by touching a long match or a grill lighter to the surface of the mixture. Watch your fingers; the alcohol flares up quickly.

4. If you're using Bridget's fire for an **Ashes** divination, now return to step 5 on page 52. To douse the fire, just cover it with a metal lid or pour water on it.

BALLOON DIAGRAMS
MAPPING YOUR MIND'S GENIUS

› BASIC ‹

Balloon diagrams are drawings that represent ideas, images, or words linked to a central concept. The neo-Platonist philosopher Porphyry of Tyros created the first-known word web of this kind in the third century CE to illustrate Aristotle's concepts. More recently, the British author Tony Buzan claims that he created contemporary mind mapping based on the concept of "general semantics" after reading about it in the science fiction novels of Robert Heinlein and A. E. van Vogt.

There are many names for this kind of mind map or "thought bubble," including spidergrams, balloon diagrams, cluster diagrams, cloud diagrams, web diagrams, word webs, or even "concept fan idea generating tool" if you use one of Edward de Bono's "lateral thinking" concepts. No matter what they're called, these webs of free association can be used to envision, generate, and organize thoughts. Like all lateral thinking and occasions of thinking outside the box, mind maps relax the rigid control of your analytical mind in order to allow your unconscious greater latitude. In terms of divination, these graphic webs can be a useful way to explore your oracular question.

Mapping Your Mind's Genius—like stream-of-consciousness writing, brainstorming, and **Repeated Cues**—is a structured form of free association. It's a visual means of eliciting and graphing any associations that bubble up from your unconscious. As science now tells us, ultimately all divinations and aha moments involve accessing remote associations.[A] Balloon diagrams just use this process in a more directed way. In fact, sometimes a balloon diagram maps out the tangents your mind takes until you hit upon a new idea.

mapping your mind's genius:
creating a visual map of your issue
will shed new light on it.

WHERE — Anywhere

WHEN — Anytime

HOW — Sitting

TOOLS — A piece of paper that's at least
8½" by 11" (21.5 × 28 cm)

A pen or pencil, or crayons of various colors

I've adapted mind mapping as a divination method for issues that have many facets. Using a balloon diagram to visually represent the ways in which these aspects interconnect or diverge will help you imagine new ways of dealing with their complications. And balloon diagrams have an additional advantage: They are nonlinear, intuitive, and non-hierarchical in nature. They allow a person to brainstorm and visualize an issue or topic by generating associations.

Since the associations are displayed radially—like branches and twigs on a tree—one association is not depicted as more important than any other. The freedom of such a sketch allows your mind to bring apparently unconnected ideas into relationship with each other and as a result, discover an insight trigger to new understanding. Therefore, they function well as visual divinations.

STEPS

1. Collect your tools.

2. Formulate your question (p. 12).

3. Ground and center (p. 15). Let your meditation create a space separate from your everyday life and a mind-set free of your ordinary, analytical thinking.

4. Begin by placing a shortened form of your query (or an image representing it) inside an oval in the center of your sheet of paper.

5. Above, below, or next to this oval, write down one major association with the issue. Draw a circle around it and connect it with a line to the central question.

6. Write down a second major association—above, below, or to the side of the original oval. Circle it and connect it to the central question. Write down third and fourth major associations in the same way and keep free-associating until an initial set of major associations has bubbled up from your unconscious. (See chapter 1, p. 18, for more information about free association.)

7. Free-associate with each of these in turn, adding smaller ovals or circles like constellations connected to the major associations. The result is a map of sorts.

8. Once you're done, add color if you want and then look over your map and see how your associations interconnect or diverge from each other—as in my personal example on page 59. Interpret your map in light of your question, using free association (p. 18) if necessary.

9. Thank your balloon diagram for your divination.

CONTINUING THE JOURNEY

Honor your oracle by displaying the **Balloon Diagram** you created in a place where you can look at it from time to time. Acknowledging your inner wisdom in this way will strengthen your connection with it.

The best way to describe the creation of a balloon diagram is to offer a personal example. Look at the balloon diagram on page 59. You can see that my original question was, "What do I need right now to be happy?" This appears in the center as "Nancy's Needs for Happiness." I then listed my major needs in the surrounding ovals: significant work, health, love, sex, peace/meditation, and play. I freely associated with each of these needs in turn, creating the balloon diagram you see on this page. I also used color to distinguish the various levels (query, major associations, associations with the major associations) of my mind map. You may want to use color, too, since it really stimulates your visual imagination.

I learned a number of things from creating this balloon diagram. I realized that my commitment to writing this book had reduced the time available to me for singing, teaching, workshops, and storytelling. This could have led to job dissatisfaction and unhappiness if I hadn't reframed my understanding of my work in some way.

I also discovered that any work I viewed as creative included a component of play. This came as good news to me, especially since I was raised to think of work as serious business and play as unnecessary, frivolous, and—as a young person—even sinful. This divination told me that I needed to recognize my writing as the creative endeavor it actually was. Leaving this mind map on my desk for several days as an "object of inner wisdom" (see p. 20 for more on objects of inner wisdom) helped me to remember and reconnect with what I had learned.

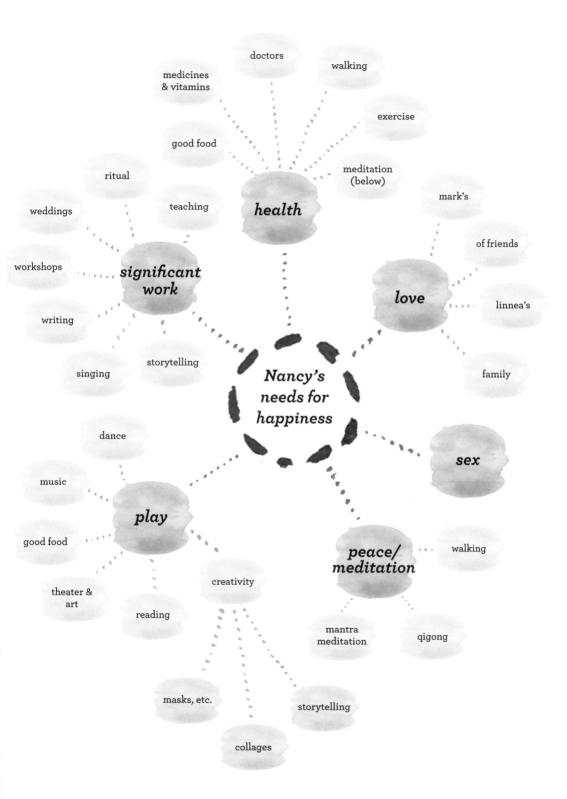

BOOKS
A FORTUITOUS WORD

› BASIC ‹

Book divinations can be dated back to at least ancient Greek times, when people interpreted poetry—preferably from the *Iliad* or the *Odyssey*—as oracles. Romans favored Virgil's *Aeneid* for their divinations and inscribed its verses on disks or tablets called *sortes*. In imperial Rome, these oracles became so renowned that *Sors* (the Latin singular of *sortes*) was added to the Goddess Fortuna's many names and titles.[B]

The ancient Hebrews used a variation on these classical methods, choosing selections from the Hebrew Bible by chance—a spiritual exercise still practiced by many Christians today. At least one bishop, St. Martin of Tours, was selected for his ecclesiastical role by using the New Testament as a guide. Similarly, Muslims derive divinatory wisdom from the *Qur'an*, while Buddhists also consult their religious texts.[B]

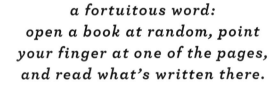

a fortuitous word:
open a book at random, point
your finger at one of the pages,
and read what's written there.

WHERE — An area with books

WHEN — Anytime

HOW — Sitting or standing

TOOLS — A book

Alternately, other printed matter

Bibliomancy, derived from the Greek for "book" (*biblio*) and "divination" (*mancy*), can be a quick and easy method for obtaining oracular guidance. In order to answer a divinatory question, you simply select a passage from a book at random. Depending on the text you use—from poetry to magazines to the Bible or your favorite novel—such an oracle can serve as a poetic illustration of your current situation, a profound source of insight, or a healing vision.

STEPS

1. Collect your tools.

2. Formulate your question (p. 12).

3. Ground and center (p. 15). Let your meditation create a space separate from your everyday life and a mind-set free of your ordinary, analytical thinking.

4. Close your eyes. Open your book at random and point your finger at one of its pages.

5. Your oracle lies beneath your finger. Read the word or passage you have chosen, preferably out loud.

6. Interpret your divination, possibly using free association (p. 18).

7. Thank the word(s) you selected for your oracle.

CONTINUING THE JOURNEY

Book divinations rely on the human ability to create connections between seemingly unrelated ideas. As a form of lateral thinking—a term coined by author Edward de Bono in 1967—this type of random word(s) choice offers a stimulus for intuitions that might otherwise lie dormant. Insight triggers like these activate unconscious, deeply buried associations or can even spark brand-new thoughts.[A]

CANDLES
LIGHT ILLUMINES THE WATER

› ADVANCED ‹

Candle oracles have existed since antiquity. Reflecting the way in which the candle(s) was used, the ancients called these divinations *capnomancy* (watching for patterns made by a candle's smoke); *ceromancy* (dripping melted wax into cold water and interpreting the images created); and *lychnoscopy* (noticing the appearance, color, and movements of the candle's flame to answer an oracular question). Candle magic can also be found in Jewish and Christian contexts—especially in the Middle Ages—in the Far East (for example, in Tibet), and in today's African-American hoodoo practices.[14]

light illumines the water:
relax in a warm bath and let the
candlelight reflecting off the
water mesmerize you into a
state of mind with greater access
to your inner knowing.

WHERE — In a bathtub

WHEN — Anytime

HOW — Reclining

TOOLS — A bathtub of warm water

Candles

Because of its sensuality, **Light Illumines the Water** is a special treat. I created this technique using sensory restriction, which cuts you off from your environment and draws your focus inward, as recent research shows.[A]

STEPS

1. Collect your tools.

2. Formulate your question (p. 12).

3. Light your candles and run your bath, but fill the tub only halfway.

4. Slip into the water and ground and center (p. 15).

5. Ask your question, either in a whisper or silently in your mind.

6. Run water over your body as it fills the tub.

7. Lean back and relax in this magical environment. Watch the play of candlelight on the water. Listen to the warm water splash gently against the tub when you move. Enjoy this sensory experience and let your mind drift for ten to fifteen minutes. In some cases, you may need less time for your oracle: Remember that divination has its own timetable.

8. Return to your question and see what insights occur to you. Do the candles shed light on your question? Does your mild trance lead to new ideas?

9. Interpret your oracle, perhaps with the help of free association (p. 18).

10. Thank the candlelight (and your warm bathwater) for your divination.

CONTINUING THE JOURNEY

This technique uses three forms of sensory restriction to turn your attention inward. First, the running water produces a type of "white noise" that blocks out other sounds. Then, the warmth of the water makes it more difficult to feel the boundaries of your body. And, finally, the dim lighting limits your vision.

Make sure to only partially fill your tub before you begin. The play of running water over your hands, legs, or torso can begin the trance induction that will bring the guidance you seek. The warm water relaxing your body and the candlelight reflecting magically off its surface allow you to let go of your thoughts and enter the enlarged space of the present moment so that you can watch for your oracular answer as it reflects off the water or lights up your mind.

CREATURES
GUIDANCE FROM THE WILD

› BASIC ‹

Seers throughout the ages have used many types of animal, bird, and insect oracles in their divination. Ancient adepts observed living creatures and their behaviors to find inspiration, studying rats or mice (*myomancy*); snakes (*opiomancy*); fish (*ichthyomancy*); insects (*entomancy*); and birds (*augury* or *ornithomancy*). Classic animal oracles also crossed into the auditory realm, as with *hippomancy*, or the interpretation of the stamping and neighing of a horse.

Apantomancy, a chance meeting with an animal, offers another age-old technique that's still used today. The Celts called this divination *deuchainn* or "first sight." They sought their oracles by clambering up a hill too steep for most animals to climb, and then noticing the first creature they met on their descent.[C] **Guidance from the Wild**—my version of this divinatory technique—suggests that you simply walk in a natural area with a question in your mind: The animal, bird, or insect you notice symbolizes the intuitive knowledge you seek.

guidance from the wild:
walk through a favorite park
or natural area with a
question in mind and notice
which creature(s) you see.

WHERE — A natural area

WHEN — Daytime

HOW — Walking

TOOLS — A natural area for walking

In this divination, you accept the first creature you see as your oracle, just as the ancient Celts did when divining with "first sight." Taking a walk outside or visiting another realm in your imagination—especially one that transports you far from your everyday life—can dissipate thoughts that have become fixed in your mind. This is so-called fixation forgetting,[A] a process that allows you to entertain new ideas. As I mentioned in chapter 2, thinking is almost always associated with the contexts in which you have those thoughts. So, changing your context by getting away from your normal haunts helps you overcome your obvious "first thoughts" in order to tap into more obscure—and potentially more valuable—answers to your query. Here, the creature you see becomes an insight trigger that prompts an unconscious thought(s) to pop into your mind, suggesting an answer or solution to your question or concern.[A] (Do try to accept the very first creature you see as your oracle even if it doesn't appeal to you. After all, manipulating your divination will only cause you to miss out on new insights and self-discovery.)

STEPS

1. Collect your tools.

2. Find a natural area (park, woodland, beach, or wilderness) where you want to walk. Acknowledge this place as your source of guidance.

3. Formulate your question (p. 12).

4. Ground and center (p. 15). Let your meditation create a space separate from your everyday life and a mind-set free of your ordinary, analytical thinking.

5. State your question out loud.

6. Walk attentively, allowing a creature(s) to come into view.

7. Interpret the animal, bird, or insect, asking what this creature means to you. Use free association (p. 18) if necessary. You can also look through the lists of common North American bugs, animals, and birds found on pages 233 to 235 if you have no personal connotations for the creature you've seen.

8. Thank the creature(s) you saw for your oracle.

CONTINUING THE JOURNEY

Indigenous seers favor oracles, like **Creatures**, that occur in nature. Today, we finally understand why. Spending time outside expands our attention: It broadens the visual field, which in turn broadens thinking, one of the techniques for facilitating sudden realizations.[A]

One way of honoring this type of divination is painting or drawing the creature you encountered on your oracular walk. Taping your picture to the refrigerator or hanging it up in front of your desk will remind of you of the intuition this divination has awakened in you.

Interpreting an animal, bird, or bug sighting is often the most difficult part of this oracle. Here's why. Most of us have a good idea of what a dog or a cat symbolizes: For many people, a dog represents loyalty or a steadfast friend, while a cat, which often appears much more independent or even aloof, represents self-reliance. We also associate owls with wisdom and bees with life's sweetness, since they make honey. But to move beyond these cultural references, you often have to ponder an animal's personal meaning for you. Such a meaning might come from its habits; from stories or other portrayals of it; or simply from the impressions it leaves on you. Over time, you'll accumulate an individual symbolic vocabulary for the creatures you meet in divinations. For example, a dog barking aggressively might be a friend who has betrayed you. Or seeing an owl in daytime might represent a secret that has come to light.

To start developing your own symbolic interpretations, look at the tables on pages 233 to 235. They list some of the connotations associated with common North American animals, birds, and bugs. I've included a blank column in each table where you can record your own personal meanings. Again, it's important to remember that your individual associations—your memories, connotations, or links with a particular creature—are almost always more meaningful than general cultural interpretations when it comes to divination.

DREAMS
AWAKENING TO INSIGHT

› ADVANCED ‹

Dreaming as a form of divination has roots in many ancient cultures. Incubating a dream oracle may have originated in Egypt, as both the cults of Serapis and Isis used this oracular procedure in which the seeker would think about a specific issue prior to sleep in order to dream about it. In fact, Herodotus records the first dream oracle, which appeared to the pharaoh Sethos in the seventh century BCE.[15] Dreaming also played an integral role in curing disease among the classical Greeks, who erected over three hundred temples to the healer God Asklepios. And a number of indigenous people, including the Senoi of Malaysia and various North American Indians, have long histories of dream interpretation.

Today, many people who have no other familiarity with divination recognize that dreams can provide insight into their lives. And scientists have recently shown that dream incubation works. It brings out obscure associations embedded in a person's recollections through a process called "memory consolidation"[A]—associations that might never surface otherwise.

awakening to insight: prime yourself to dream about your oracular question and awaken to insight.

WHERE — In bed

WHEN — While sleeping

HOW — Lying down

TOOLS — Paper, plus pen or pencil to record your dream

STEPS

1. Place the paper and pen or pencil next to your bed before you go to sleep.

2. Formulate your question (p. 12).

3. If you wish, you may write it on a piece of paper and slip it under your pillow. You may also place a glass of water under your bed to help your dreams to flow. If at all possible, don't set your alarm clock: Waking up naturally helps you remember your dream.

4. Before you fall asleep, think about your question.

5. As you feel yourself beginning to drift off, repeat your question silently and ask yourself to remember your dream in the morning.

6. When you awake, record your dream right away, even if it's just a fragment that doesn't make sense. Describe it in the present tense, as if it's happening right now. If you can, write down your dream without opening your eyes. You can do this by using your nondominant hand to align your writing on the page so that your dream log actually "descends" the paper; that is, your dominant hand writes, starting at the place marked by your nondominant hand, and when it has finished a line, the nondominant hand slides down the sheet to indicate where the next line begins.

7. Interpret your dream, if necessary with free association (p. 18). See "Continuing the Journey" for methods of interpretation.

8. Thank your dream for your divination.

CONTINUING THE JOURNEY

It can be difficult to "catch" a dream before it evaporates in the morning light. In fact, sometimes it seems as if you haven't dreamed at all. If this happens, don't worry: Just write down anything that comes into your mind upon awakening. After all, your unconscious has been working on your question all night, so even if you're unable to remember a dream, it'll still have something for you when you wake up.

Once you've recorded your dream, there are a number of ways to begin interpreting it. It's easiest to ask a friend or family member to help you, or you can interpret the dream on your own. Either way, it's important to remember that characters in your dream almost always represent parts of yourself (with the exception of people who are daily presences in your life, like a spouse, partner, at-home child, or parent). If you dream of a favorite high school math teacher, for instance, ask yourself which aspect of your life he or she represents. Does this dream character embody math, numbers, learning, or teaching—or some other quality of your former teacher?

It can be useful to enlist the help of a friend or relative when deciphering the symbols in your dream. She or he will have only one job: to keep asking you, "What does that symbol represent for you?" Your job is to answer these questions repeatedly, considering each symbol, until you have an aha experience and the dream's meaning falls into place. Your helper can suggest possible interpretations, but only you will know which ones resonate. As I mentioned in chapter 1, we had a single rule in my dream group: "The dreamer knows." As the dreamer, you're ultimately the only person who can understand your dream.

You can also interpret your dream on your own. To do so, you'll need to ask yourself the same types of questions that a good listener might pose—especially the question regarding the meaning of symbols, images, and puns. One way to do this is to freely associate with one or two of the main symbols in your dream (see "Use Free Association," p. 18). You might also ask yourself about the relationship between the major images—including the people—in your dream. Or, you might inquire into the most significant feelings in the dream: This may begin to clarify it as well. Plotting the actions that occur in the dream by sketching a timeline of it is another method of unpacking its meaning. You can also ask questions about the major themes portrayed in your dream.

As with all personal symbolism, the more often you pay attention to your dreams and the images in them, the better you'll become at interpreting them. Consider keeping a personal symbol book so that you can begin to familiarize yourself with their meanings. I've kept a dream journal for many years, and I've found that, although my dreams rarely foresee the future—as they did once when I saw my yet-to-be-conceived daughter—they often inform me about issues that are surfacing in my life. This allows me to make informed decisions rather than muddling through my days, which I find much more valuable than my dreams' infrequent predictive power.

MIRRORS

REFLECTING YOUR FEELINGS

› ADVANCED ‹

Since before the invention of mirrors, reflective surfaces have played an important role in scrying, the ancient technique of looking beyond a shiny surface to detect oracular signs. Indigenous cultures have used bowls of liquid, pools of water, and fingernails covered with oil, as well as mirrors made from obsidian or other shiny materials. Most of us associate this form of divination with Snow White's evil stepmother, who asks her magic mirror, "Who's the fairest of them all?" But for an Omàmiwininì (Algonquin) seer, this practice amounts to "seeing his own soul."[C]

Before the Spanish conquest of Mexico, Mesoamerican mirrors, made from polished pieces of iron ore, pyrite, and obsidian, were viewed as sacred objects that allowed shamans to make contact with supernatural forces. In fact, during the late Aztec Empire, the entire cosmos was conceived of as a huge circular mirror, a fact that explains the mirror's spiritual importance.

The Spanish Conquistador Hernán Cortés brought an obsidian mirror back to Europe after the fall of Mexico, and John Dee, a counselor to Queen Elizabeth I and one of Europe's most famous diviners, used it for scrying. Around the same time in France, Nostradamus was reputed to use a bowl of darkened water on a tripod for the same purpose.[16]

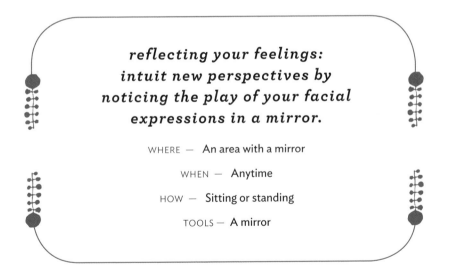

reflecting your feelings: intuit new perspectives by noticing the play of your facial expressions in a mirror.

WHERE — An area with a mirror

WHEN — Anytime

HOW — Sitting or standing

TOOLS — A mirror

Observing the changing emotions on your face can give you information about your feelings concerning your query: a glare, a frown, or a grimace may illuminate you.

STEPS

1. Decide which mirror you want to use. Acknowledge it as your source of guidance.

2. Formulate your question (p. 12).

3. Ground and center (p. 15). Let your meditation create a space separate from your everyday life and a mind-set free of your ordinary, analytical thinking.

4. State your question out loud.

5. Then, watch the emotions on your face as you think about your question.

6. Ask your question out loud again and notice any new facial expressions. Does your lip curl, indicating contempt? Do your eyes squint or roll, showing disapproval or exasperation? Do you furrow your forehead? Raise your eyebrows? Or bite a lip in fear? Do your nostrils flare in anger? Or do you smile slyly? Wince? Scowl? Frown? Your emotions about your issue will unconsciously show up on your face.

7. Keep asking your question rapidly until you've discovered your feelings about your question.

8. If after five to ten minutes you haven't received an oracle, remind yourself of your query and meditate for five more minutes.

9. Interpret your divination, perhaps with the help of free association (p. 18).

10. Thank your mirror for your oracle.

CONTINUING THE JOURNEY

I created this technique as a counterpart to **Repeated Cues**, using the visual rather than the auditory sense. Like Repeated Cues, you might have to ask your question many times before you see new possibilities. It's a good idea to repeat your query rapidly, so you don't have time to think about it, but simply react instead. After exhausting your pat "answers," you'll finally surprise yourself with a new expression that brings the issue alive for you.

NUMBERS
NUMERICAL WISDOM

› BASIC ‹

People usually view numbers as simple indicators of quantity, but the first nine digits (as well as a few other integers) also express symbolic qualities. As a result of this characteristic, single-digit numbers have carried mystical connotations for most populations in Europe, Asia, Africa, and the Americas. In fact, the Greek philosopher and mathematician Pythagoras considered numbers to be divine. Pythagoras and his followers, like Jung centuries later, ascribed special significance to the first four digits, which, when added together, produce 10, the Pythagorean number of perfection (1 + 2 + 3 + 4 = 10).[17]

Most American Indians also view numbers in a sacred light. The number 4 has an important symbolic value in many of their myths and rituals, because it represents the four directions, the four winds, the four seasons, the four stages of human life, the four kinds of living things, the four divisions of time, and so on. The Anishinaabe (Ojibway) recognize many of these sets of four and also believe that four powers compose the physical world—wind, water, fire, and rock—and that four great teachers came to earth, bringing with them their wisdom and medicine.[18]

This qualititive or symbolic character of numbers prompted me to create the oracular technique **Numerical Wisdom**. First, you select a number, and then you use its symbolic connotations as a catalyst for tapping into your deeper self. Science has now demonstrated that such insight triggers have the ability to call up new thoughts from a person's unconscious.[A]

numerical wisdom:
create a deck of number cards,
then choose one as your divination.

WHERE — Anywhere

WHEN — Anytime

HOW — Sitting or standing

TOOLS — A deck of number cards

When I began to work with the magic of numbers, I cut out ten cards and printed each of the integers from 0 through 9 on them so that I could use them like tarot cards or a set of runes. You can also use the ace through nine from a deck of playing cards for the integers 1 through 9 and a joker to represent "0."

You may want to augment your deck with the numbers 10, 11, 12, 13, 22, 33, and 40. This is because the first nine integers, plus 10–13, 22, 33, and 40, all have cultural associations. Since our numerical system—the so-called decimal system—is based on the number 10, it carries a lot of weight in Western society. Twelve also has great significance in Anglo-Saxon societies. In fact, it may have been the basis for an earlier number system, especially when it comes to measurement: Think 12 inches to a foot; a dozen doughnuts; or 12 months to the year. And 13 may have predated 12 when it comes to the calendar, since there are 13 lunar months in the year, and the lunar calendar predated the solar. Still, most people in North America consider it an unlucky number. And 40 has many biblical associations, including the length of the flood in days and the number of days and nights Jesus spent in the desert during his temptation by the devil.

Modern numerologists consider 11, 22, and 33 to be master numbers. According to numerological lore, these numbers intensify or deepen the quality of the integer to which they can be reduced by adding their two digits together. For instance, 33 represents an intensification of the number 6 (since adding the two digits together, we get 3 + 3 = 6); that is, the more elevated or spiritual aspects of this single-digit number. The concept of 22 as the most powerful master number or "master builder" has several roots: The Hebrew alphabet has twenty-two letters, the major arcana contains twenty-two cards, and there are twenty-two pathways within Kabbalah.

Each of the master numbers connotes intuition and spirituality. With the exception of the numbers 11 and 22, when your question involves more mundane (that is, not spiritual) aspects of your life, you can add up the digits of the master number and reduce it to its single-digit equivalent. But in most cases, master numbers point to your potential for spiritual growth and understanding.

As a springboard for understanding the number you pick from your deck, I'm including a list of some of the most widely accepted numerical associations in the Appendix (p. 236). But if any number has personal connotations for you, those will almost always be more significant than the ones I've suggested: For example, when I receive the number 4, it sometimes points to the fact that I am one of four sisters.

STEPS

1. Collect your number cards. Place them facedown on a flat surface or inside a container, so you don't see which number you're choosing. Acknowledge them as your source of guidance.

2. Formulate your question (p. 12).

3. Ground and center (p. 15). Let your meditation create a space separate from your everyday life and a mind-set free of your ordinary, analytical thinking.

4. Select one of the cards.

5. Interpret the card you receive, using your own connotations with that number, the "Numerical Associations" table (see p. 236), or free association (p. 18), if necessary.

6. Thank your number for your oracle.

CONTINUING THE JOURNEY

Playing with possible numerical meanings can be fun, enchanting, and illuminating: Numbers often point toward ages, historical dates, measurements, prices, clothes sizes, TV channels, temperatures, populations, and so on. For example, the next time you go to the grocery store to pick up a few items and your bill adds up to $17.76, remember the Declaration of Independence and the beginning of the American Revolution. It may simply light up your day or liberate you in some way; it may remind you of your own freedom and independence in a part of your life that feels constricted; or, it may be a sign that you need to exercise that independence more. Or, perhaps you see a license plate inscribed with 986. Adding a decimal point, you might think of good health, since 98.6°F (37°C) is optimal body temperature. In either case, the number you notice will probably offer you a good omen.

SCRYING

GAZING INTO YOUR INNER WELL

› ADVANCED ‹

Scrying is an ancient technique for looking beyond the surface of any reflective object to detect signs from deep within. The term is derived from the obsolete form of the word descry, meaning "discovery or view from afar."

Most of us associate this divination method with two fictional characters: Snow White's evil stepmother and the Wicked Witch of the West, who watches as her flying monkeys attack Dorothy in *The Wizard of Oz*. In the rest of the world, people honor scrying as a method for accessing "second sight," the kind of vision that allows people to see more deeply within themselves and envision their inner wisdom.

Science has now shown that such internal focus often immediately precedes creative insight, since it minimizes the distractions that can block an unconscious idea or image from emerging.[A] In this way, **Gazing into Your Inner Well** will connect you with your own inner wisdom.

gazing into your inner well:
stare at water with a soft focus for
five to ten minutes or until an answer
to your question surfaces.

WHERE — Anywhere private

WHEN — Anytime

HOW — Sitting or standing

TOOLS — Clear water in either a transparent
container or a bowl

Scrying depends on the ability to unfocus your eyes and look deeply into your unconscious using your mind's eye: You're not actually looking *at* the water or other reflective surface, but gazing through it or within it. Some people find it's easier to do this in a darkened room or by looking toward the water from an angle.

STEPS

1. Formulate your question (p. 12).

2. Collect your tools.

3. Ground and center (p. 15). Let your meditation create a space separate from your everyday life and a mind-set free of your ordinary, analytical thinking.

4. State your question out loud.

5. Use peripheral vision, allowing your eyes to unfocus and gaze beyond the surface of your oracular water. The surface of the water may begin to change, becoming misty or fogged over.

6. Look through or within the water or mist so that your inner eyes can see visualizations, symbols, or images that give you insight into your oracular question. The mild trance induced by peripheral vision will allow oracular images like still photographs or even mini-movies to swim into view.

7. Scry in this way for five to ten minutes, or until you see an image.

8. Interpret your oracle, perhaps with the help of free association (p. 18).

9. Thank the water for your oracle.

CONTINUING THE JOURNEY

If you're an auditory or kinesthetic diviner like I am, performing **Scrying** may work, but differently than it does for someone who's visual. Recently, I tried to scry, but after gazing at the water for several minutes, the telephone roused me from my trance. Although the message was for my husband, I knew immediately that it was also meant for me. I discovered two important things from this experience: First, when something interrupts a divination, it becomes part of the oracle. And second, I recognized that if you're auditory in your divinatory proclivities like I am, you may very well hear your answer even if you employ a visual oracle.

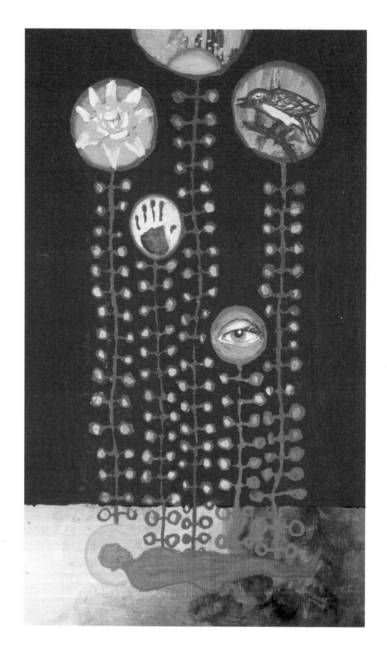

SPIRIT GUIDES
INNER JOURNEY FOR GUIDANCE

› ADVANCED ‹

Spirit guides come in many forms: guardian angels, saints, animal or bird spirits, tree guides, deceased relatives, or enlightened individuals, as well as Gods, or Goddesses, depending on which religious tradition you examine. In Taiwan, for example, Taoist priests call on spirit helpers—including the pole stars, local deities, and the spirit of the soil—to cure sick individuals, while in Japan, the minor Shinto *kami* (spirits) or ancestral spirits can sometimes act as unseen helpers.[D]

In the West, the beliefs of theosophists and spiritualists embrace spirit guides, as do people who rely on guardian angels for help and guidance. Indigenous traditions the world over employ spirit guides, especially when they perform shamanic journeys as a means of divination. Recently, anthropologist Michael Harner reexamined these divinatory practices and discovered many similarities among the various traditions, including rapid drumming, ritual dance, and communication with a person's power animal or spirit guide. He distilled these methods into an oracular technique called core shamanism that now has thousands of proponents in North America. In this oracle, you'll consult your own spirit guide for insight into your divinatory question.

inner journey for guidance:
enter the wisdom of the
spirit world by following the lead
of your spirit guide.

WHERE — Anywhere private

WHEN — Anytime

HOW — Lying down or sitting comfortably

TOOLS — Someone to drum for you or
a recording of shamanic drumming
(See "Drumming," in Resources, p. 226)

A partner to monitor your trance

Until recently, shamanic journeying was only practiced within indigenous cultures by men and women who had special sensitivities and gifts. But in its current form, this technique has expanded to include many "ordinary" people. Shamanic trance can be quite deep, so until you have journeyed a number of times, it's a good idea to work with a partner. As you enter trance, your partner monitors your journey to make sure that you return to a normal waking state after you're done.

Shamanic journeying relies on several scientifically proven techniques. Like dreaming, the shamanic journey involves an altered state of consciousness in which novel ideas can be incubated from a pre-trance question. The trance state (see chapter 1, p. 16) generates a "brain blink" that allows an unconscious rearrangement of thoughts leading to fresh ideas. And visiting another realm in your imagination also means a change of context, another scientifically tested strategy for inducing an aha moment.[A]

Shamanic journeying is an imaginative process much like daydreaming: You close your eyes, become relaxed, and drift off into another world. The steady heartbeat rhythm of shamanic drumming helps you float into an altered state of mind, in which you imagine a world much like our own—a world known among core shamanism practitioners as the "lower world."[19] Here, you meet a creature of some sort. Often called your power animal, this being will escort you on an adventure that will help you find insight into your question.

Visualizations like this one can revise your understanding of the issue that has prompted you to perform an oracle. When you take an **Inner Journey for Guidance**, your unconscious gives new shape to your way of thinking through the images that arise: The story of your journey, the habitats you see, the sounds your hear, and the characters you meet are all symbols that your unconscious creates to give your conscious mind insights into your query. Your spirit guide's words also cast light on your oracular question. And once you're done, it's a matter of deciphering the symbolic landscape of your journey (see chapter 1, p. 18).

To reach the lower world in your imagination, you need to visualize yourself entering a natural crevice, like a hollow tree, a fault in a rock face, or a natural spring. From there, you'll often travel a circuitous path inside the earth: Sometimes you'll hear a voice telling you which way to go, and after much meandering, you'll arrive. If you don't already have a spirit guide, your first journey will have a dual purpose: to discover your spirit helper and to answer your question.

When your partner indicates that your journey is almost over (say, with one minute to go), you should retrace your path through the earth to the crevice, spring, or tree stump where you began. When you've reemerged from the earth, slowly open your eyes and record your journey.

STEPS

1. Formulate your question (p. 12).

2. Discuss a time limit for your shamanic journey with your partner: say, five to ten minutes for the first time.

3. Decide how you will imaginatively enter the earth: through a rock crevice, a sinkhole, a spring, a tree stump, or whatever resonates with you. Sometimes it helps to visualize a natural place you know well.

4. Lie on your back or sit comfortably in a chair with your head fully supported.

5. Ground and center (p. 15). Let your meditation create a space separate from your everyday life and a mind-set free of your ordinary, analytical thinking.

6. Have your partner begin drumming or begin your recording of drum sounds.

7. When the drumming begins, enter the earth in your imagination and travel down, down, down, until you find yourself in the lower world. See yourself winding through damp tunnels lined with stone or packed dirt. Feel the coolness of the air as you descend into Mother Earth.

8. Once you've entered the lower world, look around. Are you in a meadow? A forest? Next to a lake, stream, or beach? Or in a desert? Gaze at the landscape and locate yourself here. Notice the plants and animals, and the contours of the land. Is it hilly or mountainous? Flat and barren? Or lush and tropical? Do you

hear birdsong? A cascading brook or crashing waves? The cries of an animal?

9. Take in the sights and sounds of the lower world until a creature approaches. When an animal, a bird, or an insect greets you, ask if it's your spirit guide. If it answers "no," continue wandering through the lower world, noticing everything around you.

10. Once a creature acknowledges that it's your spirit guide, thank him or her politely for coming to your aid. Then ask your divinatory question. Listen to the answer, but also watch where your power animal takes you and what it does.

11. When your partner tells you your time is almost up—say, a minute or so left—or speeds up the drumbeat to indicate the end of your journey, thank your spirit helper and retrace your path through the earth back to your entry point into the lower world.

12. Slowly open your eyes and interpret your oracle, perhaps with help from your partner or with free association (p. 18).

CONTINUING THE JOURNEY

Spirit guides may come to you in many ways. For example, if you often dream of a particular bird, bug, or animal—especially if it figures in your dream life as a guide or a protector—it may be a sign that this being is one of your spirit helpers. In fact, you can also use a **Dream** divination (see p. 72) to discover the identity of a guardian spirit. Sometimes these spirit guides help within the context of a particular situation; sometimes they will accompany you for years; and sometimes they become lifelong companions.

You can also adopt a spirit guide by reading about Gods and Goddesses, power animals, saints, enlightened masters, or guardian angels, paying special attention to those who embody qualities that you need or want to develop. Such study may reveal a number of guides who feel right to you.

Although adopting a spiritual guide through reading is a conscious process, you will probably begin to trust your inner wisdom to eventually reveal spirit guides to you. In fact, some guardian spirits may announce their significance in your life through events or circumstances, and especially through synchronicities, bringing themselves to your attention again and again.

An **Inner Journey for Guidance** can be a dramatic experience that often includes an elaborate narrative, very like a dream. During your initial encounter with your spirit guide on such a journey, it's important to spend much of your time getting to know its essential qualities: where it lives, what supports its life, what it loves. You can do this by asking it questions and observing how it acts. Later, when you've returned to your normal reality, you can also read about the power animal you've met. This information will help you interpret your inner journey.

It's also important to integrate the guidance you receive on your Inner Journey for Guidance in a thoughtful manner. Act on your spirit guide's counsel. Make the changes he or she suggests. Once you have done that, you can journey again for further advice. Your travels to the lower world provide an evocative source of personal stories and symbolism that you can learn from for weeks, months, or even years. Shamanic journeys can be powerful experiences. Let them simmer for a while.

You can also honor the help you've received from your spirit guide by checking in with it in the future. Your power animal loves to assist you, but it needs you to request its aid. You can do this by simply asking for help, preferably out loud, and then opening your senses for an answer—listening, watching, or feeling into its guidance. It might even be a good idea to ask for its assistance with specific goals, whether they're daily, weekly, or even monthly objectives or aims.

STARS
COSMIC CONNECT-THE-DOTS

› ADVANCED ‹

Gazing at the sky for omens may be the oldest and most widespread oracle in existence. Ancient astrologers and soothsayers paid attention to the sky because they found their lives reflected in the moon, sun, planets, and stars. The study of the stars—*astro* (stars) plus *logia* (study)—evolved independently in many parts of the world. In China, for instance, the emperor trusted a group of bureaucrats called Pao-chang to read the heavens for signs that might affect the land.[C] The ancient Egyptians established the first form of astrology that used a person's birth date to determine their personality, and by the third century BCE, the ancient Greeks had developed the system of astrology that's still used in the United States and Europe, basing it largely on the earlier work of Babylonian and Egyptian astrologers.[E] At about the same time in India, sages had already codified astrology, focusing especially on cataclysmic events by observing comets, shooting stars, and lunar and solar eclipses. Stargazing also played a part in the divination systems of Guatemala and Peru as far back as the Aztec, Mayan, and Incan civilizations.[E] In this oracle, you'll look heavenward—just as our ancestors did—in order to trace a pattern in the stars.

cosmic connect-the-dots:
after going outside at night, notice
which quadrant of the sky calls to you
and what image(s) you see there.

WHERE — Outside

WHEN — Night

HOW — Sitting or standing

TOOLS — The sky at night

Paper and pen or pencil

Astrology can provide oracular information, but the sky itself can answer your divinatory questions, too. **Cosmic Connect-the-Dots**[20] works particularly well if you find yourself in the country, where you can see lots of stars. Don't worry if you're not familiar with the names and shapes of constellations: You'll still be able to discover your own star patterns in the sky. In fact, connecting the stars like a dot-to-dot puzzle resembles the process involved in solving the Nine-Dot Problem (see below, left). This famous brainteaser gave rise to the phrase "thinking outside the box"—which is exactly what you want to do in order to facilitate creative insight. The task for this paper-and-pencil puzzle was to connect all nine dots with no more than four straight lines, and without lifting your pencil or retracing any marks. The only way to solve it was to draw the lines outside of the box implied by the dots (see below, right).[A] Generating your own star pattern uses the same kind of creativity and primes your mind for outside-the-box thinking.

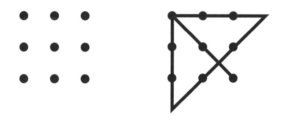

STEPS

1. Collect your tools.

2. Formulate your question (p. 12).

3. Go to the place where you'll perform the divination.

4. Acknowledge the stars as your oracle.

5. Ground and center with your eyes closed (p. 15). Let your meditation create a space separate from your everyday life and a mind-set free of your ordinary, analytical thinking.

6. Open your eyes and let them draw your attention toward one part of the sky.

7. Scan that area and then sketch the quadrant of the sky that your inner wisdom has asked you to view. Connect the dots in your stellar diagram in order to create an image or images. Like

constellation charts, your illustration may be a rough approxi-
mation of an object or a person. What does your oracular image
look like to you? Is it a geometrical shape? Does it resemble an
animal? What does this image remind you of?

8. Identify and interpret the guidance you've received, perhaps
    with the help of free association (p. 18).

9. Thank the stars for your oracle.

CONTINUING THE JOURNEY

Even if you know quite a few constellations, when you undertake a **Cosmic
Connect-the-Dots** oracle, you'll often end up linking stars in your sketch as if
they were a dot-to-dot pattern. This means you'll create an image that's unique
to your divination. Or, you may occasionally notice a constellation. In that case,
instead of working with an image that you've discovered, you can use the myth
connected with the constellation to interpret your oracle. If, for example, you
notice the Pleiades, you will probably realize that you need the help of either your
biological or metaphorical sisters, since this constellation represents seven sisters that Zeus supposedly transformed into stars. Or, if you graduated from one
of the "seven sisters" colleges, this constellation might point you in that direction.
Or, if you spot Canis Major (the dog constellation), you can ask yourself if your
issue concerns loyalty, since dogs display conspicuous loyalty when it comes to
their owners.

Of course, if you have personal connections with the constellation that
catches your eye, those associations supersede the Greek mythology normally
attributed to it. For instance, I have a friend who asserts that in a past life she
lived on a planet in the Pleiades. If she were drawn to that constellation, it might
indicate that she was dealing with that part of her personal history.

If, somehow, you've been drawn to this divination technique on a cloudy
night, the cloud cover itself might represent an oracle in its own right. It could
indicate that you're still not able to see your issue clearly, or that your vision is
shrouded in some way. Ask yourself what might be blocking your ability to view
your issue. Once this obstacle has been removed, you can return to a Cosmic
Connect-the-Dots oracle for further enlightenment.

4

AUDITORY

TECHNIQUES

THE WORD ORACLE COMES from the Latin *orare*, meaning "to speak," possibly because auditory oracles—ones that speak in words, sounds, or music—were favorites of the Greeks and Romans. They valued *augury* (listening to a bird for wisdom); *cledons* (random snippets of conversation that gave divinatory insight); the oracular sounds from the leaves of the oak tree in the sacred grove at Dodona; and, of course, the famous Oracle of Delphi. Similarly, the auditory oracles gathered in this chapter involve listening either with your external ears to sounds in your surroundings or with your inner ears to the "still, small voice within." You'll find that both can be wonderful sources of guidance.

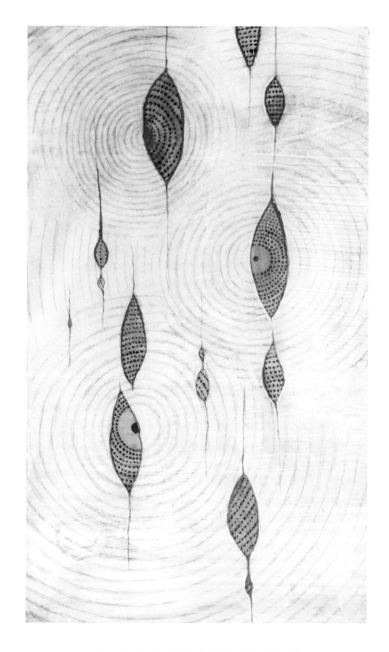

ANCESTORS

CONTACTING AN ELDER

› ADVANCED ‹

Practices honoring the dead are performed by ancient and indigenous cultures all over the world, both in everyday life and within religion. Ancestor worship makes up the single most important religious activity in China. And across the Far East, homage to ancestral spirits upholds the social order and reminds the living of their responsibilities to their next of kin. American Indians of both North and South America also esteem the older members of their community as well as those who have passed on. Just think of the festive celebration of Dia de los Muertos in Mexico, for instance.[D]

In the West, worshipping ancestors is a foreign concept. For some people, it might even conjure up images of ghosts and apparitions. Death remains one of our major taboos in North America, and that makes contacting an ancestor more complicated for us than for those in other cultures.

But it wasn't always this way. In pre-Christian Europe, people believed that during the transition from fall to winter, the veils between the worlds of the living and the dead were at their thinnest. For that reason, on the nights surrounding the ancient celebration of Samhain or Hallowmas, early Europeans invited their ancestors to join them as their guests, often setting places at the table for them.

If you remember how dearly your departed grandmother loved you (or perhaps another family member), the reason for contacting a dead relative becomes immediately apparent: Beloved elders wanted the best for us in life and continue to do so after death. Your love for them can become a portal for your divination, since it's one of the positive emotions that facilitate eureka moments.[A]

contacting an elder: encourage a deceased loved one to offer you guidance about an issue.

WHERE — **Anywhere private**

WHEN — **Anytime**

HOW — **Sitting or lying down**

TOOLS — **None**

Like people all over the world, you can encourage a deceased family member to commune with you about an issue that's confusing you. If your ancestry is European, it might be especially appropriate to do this during the shift from autumn to winter, or on a special date that holds memories of your departed loved one.

Remember that if your ancestor does not answer you within ten or fifteen minutes, he or she may still contact you in the days, weeks, or even months that follow. This type of divination always remains a two-way street, since it involves a partnership between two people. You may hear from certain deceased relatives only once or not at all, since some souls seem to gravitate away from their former lives more quickly than others.

STEPS

1. Formulate a question for your beloved ancestor (p. 12).

2. Decide where you want to perform your divination—perhaps in a place where your loved one enjoyed spending time.

3. Ground and center (p. 15). Let your meditation create a space separate from your everyday life and a mind-set free of your ordinary, analytical thinking.

4. Keep your eyes closed and silently ask that one of your departed loved ones join you in thinking about your oracular question. Imagine this elder in your mind's eye or gaze at a photo of your ancestor. You may also hold an object that reminds you of your departed loved one: a ring or childhood toy, for example. If you like, you might add that only someone who has your best interests at heart is welcome.

5. Imagine your elder sitting opposite you. See his face. Notice her clothing. Bring him or her to mind as vividly as possible. Then, ask your question and listen for your ancestor's voice or for other

sounds that respond to your query. Sit quietly for ten to fifteen minutes or until an answer comes.

6. Interpret your oracle, perhaps with the help of free association (p. 18).

7. Thank your ancestor for your oracle.

CONTINUING THE JOURNEY

You can ask a specific ancestor to speak with you about your issue; or, alternatively, you may send out a call for any person who has loved you during his or her lifetime. Those who respond to your requests for help will be people who loved you or had a strong positive regard for you while alive. If adding a precautionary statement, as suggested in step 4, makes you feel safe, then by all means add it. Feeling safe is a prerequisite for any successful divination.

Here's a personal example. I "speak" with my maternal grandmother and my father (both of whom have died) about once a year—usually on their birth or death dates—because I appreciate the wisdom they have for me. They have both had helpful insights that they conveyed to me as words that I heard in my mind.

Occasionally, a distant predecessor will also contact me, as a Mohawk ancestress once did while I was writing a book about indigenous mythology. (Stories passed down in the Vedder family indicate that we're descended from two *Kanien'kehaka*, or Mohawk, women who married Dutch colonists named Vedder in the seventeenth century.) She told me that my book was a gift from her people to mine, blessing my desire to share native wisdom with a mostly white audience.

Communication with the dead can also occur through synchronicities and dreams; for instance, when a deceased loved one's favorite animal pops up on the sidewalk in front of you or when you hear her favorite song on the radio. After my friend Abbie died, she sent a good-bye message by rattling the doorknob to the room in our home where she'd temporarily lived before moving out of town. And at the time of his death, my father came to me in a dream to let me know of his passing. I saw his golden spirit rising from his body, and fifteen minutes later the phone rang to let us know that he had died.

BIRDS
AVIAN ADVICE

› ADVANCED ‹

Are you wondering if it's an auspicious time for a wedding, a party, or other affair? If so, ask the birds. After all, they gave their name to the word *auspicious*, which comes from the Latin *avis spex*, meaning "blessed by a bird sighting." If you want to select the right day for your event, you can perform an augury, which translates as "bird telling" from the Latin. As these terms indicate, the Romans held bird oracles in high esteem—so much so that Julius Caesar appointed himself head of the official group of augurs when he came to power.[B]

Avian divinations comprise some of the most ancient oracular practices known to humanity. Germanic tribes watched the flight of birds, as did the Jaqi (Aymara) Indians in South America, the ancient Slavs, the desert Arabs during Mohammed's time, and people in northwest China today. The ancient Incas listened attentively to birdsong, as did the Sakha (Yakut) people in Siberia, the Wyandot (Hurons) in North America, the Aborigines in Australia, and the Iban people of Borneo.[C]

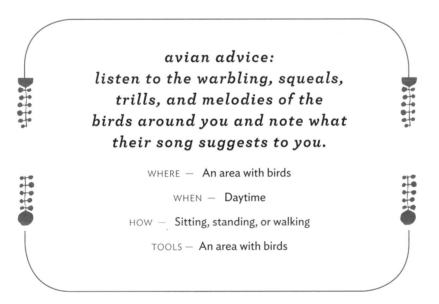

avian advice:
listen to the warbling, squeals,
trills, and melodies of the
birds around you and note what
their song suggests to you.

WHERE — An area with birds

WHEN — Daytime

HOW — Sitting, standing, or walking

TOOLS — An area with birds

Avian Advice as a divinatory method has less to do with identifying birds than with listening to their songs. For that reason, this oracle feels much like listening to waves (see **Ripples of Truth** on p. 154). As you notice the rhythm and melody of the bird's chorus, it begins to evoke words in your mind. If you're like me, you'll probably hear your oracle as speech—but it might also come as a melody or a sound of another sort.

STEPS

1. Determine where you want to listen to birdsong, preferably in a place where you will hear a number of calls, such as a park, a nature sanctuary, or even the aviary at the local zoo. Acknowledge this place as your source of guidance.

2. Formulate your question (p. 12).

3. Ground and center (p. 15). Let your meditation create a space separate from your everyday life and a mind-set free of your ordinary, analytical thinking.

4. Close your eyes and silently ask your question.

5. Listen to the birds' song until words or other sounds begin to form in your mind. Let their trills, peeps, chirps, squawks, warbles, and quavers infuse your senses until you slip into a light trance (see chapter 1, p. 16). Notice the rhythms of the birds' calls as they overlap and intersect. Do these sounds hint at a sentence in your mind? Does a call evoke a particular word? Or do a series of cries suggest a certain phrase? Is the birds' chatter a conversation? Listen in.

6. Do the melodies you hear remind you of anything? Are they shrill and raucous, implying conflict of some sort? Or sweet and mellow, indicating a more amicable settlement of your issue? Do the birds whistle, suggesting that they're asking for your attention? Are the whistles loud or soft? What does this signify for you? Listen for five to ten minutes or until you have your answer.

7. If after ten minutes you haven't received oracular guidance, meditate for five minutes and then restate your question and listen for a minute more.

8. Interpret your oracle. In some cases, analyzing what you've heard will involve free association (p. 18).

9. Thank the birds that sang for your oracle.

CONTINUING THE JOURNEY

Unlike a **Water** divination, **Avian Advice** doesn't involve an ongoing stream of sound. As a result, you'll have to pull together the bits and pieces of birdsong that you hear and remember what their sounds elicit for you. If it helps to write down what you've heard in your mind, take a pencil and paper with you. However, if this interrupts your trance—as it would for me—then trust your memory to retain what you've learned.

Most people in present-day North America view birds' ability to fly as a symbol for spiritual and creative activities. Like other symbols of creativity, focusing on birds may help to loosen any unnecessary restrictions on your thinking and allow new ideas to form.[A] Let your bird oracle be carried on "wings of song"—that is, conjuring an uplifting feeling—or be a "flight of fancy," stimulating your imagination. Birds represent freedom as well as human longings, so it's no wonder that they carry oracular messages.

CHANTING

SINGING THE MYSTERY AWAKE

› ADVANCED ‹

Almost every culture on earth has discovered the spiritual properties of song, and many of them have devised whole systems for tapping into these qualities. The Hindus in India, for instance, fashioned various ragas—specific scales, rhythmic patterns, and melodies—to facilitate moods at different hours of the day. The ancient Greeks formulated at least seven musical modes (like our major and minor keys) that the early medieval church adapted to immerse its flocks in the Christian sacraments. The Taoists in China, the Sufis of the Middle East, and Buddhists in many parts of the world have all performed simple chants to allow their adherents a mystical experience through music.

All over the world, chant forms a part of religious services, from the Hindu "om" to Native American drumming and chanting to the "dreamlines" of the Aboriginal Australians. Chanting allows people to be more receptive to the divine, and it constitutes a type of meditation that invites chanters into the stillness within. Chanting with either of these possibilities in mind will give you access to your deeper wisdom.

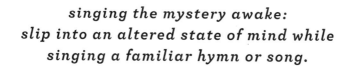

singing the mystery awake:
slip into an altered state of mind while
singing a familiar hymn or song.

WHERE — **A quiet place**

WHEN — **Anytime**

HOW — **Sitting or standing**

TOOLS — **A quiet place where your chanting won't be interrupted**

Songs that feel profound or sacred can relax you into that deep place from which you contact your intuition. A **Chanting** divination works best if you already know the song. You can drift quickly into a light trance (see chapter 1, p. 16) without thinking about what you're singing. It also helps if the melody is simple and the lyrics are easy to remember. However, you do need a strong affinity with the words, so that they will support you on your inward journey. On page 111, you will find hymns and sacred songs from many religious paths (including atheism) to use while chanting. Once you've chosen one, select a line, or at most a verse, to sing over and over. Another way of finding a chant that works for you is to notice what sounds you make when you're spontaneously experiencing delight or wonder.[F] Chanting those sounds will open you up to greater knowing.

Singing requires a healthy alignment of the body, with your head buoyant at the end of the spine, while your tailbone sinks down as if attached to the earth for stability. Chanting in this posture opens up your lungs, allowing your breathing to become longer, deeper, and finer—exactly the qualities that lead to an altered state of consciousness. You'll find that the alpha waves you experience in this meditative state open you to greater clarity about your issue.[A]

Although most people discover their inner guidance after chanting, it may also come to you before or even while you sing. When you enter the silence before or after singing, you often experience a profound shift in mental state. In this state of mind—a light trance—your innermost thoughts frequently reveal themselves to you, opening you to the wisdom within. As my friend Lorin Roche writes, "[T]he silence before you think or say the sound and the vibrant silence after you think or utter the sound are gateways."[F] If you don't experience an opening to your inner truth, chant again the following day.

STEPS

1. Decide on an appropriate hymn or sacred song to chant.

2. Find a quiet place to sing.

3. Formulate your question (p. 12).

4. Ground and center (p. 15). Let your meditation create a space separate from your everyday life and a mind-set free of your ordinary, analytical thinking.

5. State your question out loud, close your eyes, and begin to chant.

6. As you sing, feel the sound vibrating in your belly, your chest, and your head. Notice how you respond to the rhythms of your chosen song, becoming more and more centered as you connect

with the pulse of your chant. Enjoy the melody, relaxing into its contours as it rises and falls. Sing until you slip into a light trance (see chapter 1, p. 16), usually five to ten minutes.

7. Let the repetition of the song lull you into an even deeper state of altered consciousness until you get lost in the music. You may hear your guidance in the stillness that follows and precedes each repetition. Or you may become so entranced that you forget your question until suddenly an answer reveals itself.

8. When you've chanted for ten to fifteen minutes, stop singing and listen for your oracle, if it hasn't already arrived.

9. Interpret the outcome, perhaps with free association (p. 18).

10. Thank the music for your oracle.

SUGGESTIONS FOR CHANTING

If you have a favorite hymn or spiritual song, use it instead of these chants. They are grouped by faith traditions, but you may be attracted to a song from any religion. See page 226, for more information.

CHRISTIAN: "Amazing Grace"; the "Doxology" ("Praise God from whom all blessings flow"); "Nearer My God to Thee"

ROMAN CATHOLIC: "Dona Nobis Pacem" (Grant Us Peace)

PROTESTANT: "O God, Our Help in Ages Past;" "Kum Ba Yah"

QUAKER: "My Life Flows on in Endless Song"

AFRICAN-AMERICAN (AND CHRISTIAN): "Every Time I Feel the Spirit;" "Over My Head;" or other spirituals

JEWISH: "Shalom Chaverim;" "Hashiveinu;" or any niggun

MUSLIM: Any "Bismillah" or "Kalama" selection in *Spiritual Dance and Walk*

BUDDHIST: "Gate, Gate;" "Kwan Zeon Bosai" in *Spiritual Dance and Walk*

HINDU: "Om Nama Shivaya"

PAGAN OR WICCAN: "Touching Her Deep;" "Spiraling into the Center"

NATIVE AMERICAN: "Ungawa" (Chumash); "We Are One" (Arapaho)

ATHEIST: "'Tis the Gift to Be Simple;" "This Little Light of Mine;" "Rise Up, O Flame"

DIVINE INSPIRATION

DIALOGUE WITH THE SACRED

› BASIC ‹

The term *divination* derives from the same root as the word *divine*. In its original meaning, divination consisted of direct contact with a deity and, as such, has occurred in all cultures and in all eras. Divine inspiration—literally, breathing in the sacred—is a good synonym for such a **Dialogue with the Sacred**.

In the West, prayer serves as the best-known means of communicating with God. Christians, Muslims, and Jews practice this type of Dialogue with the Sacred. Many American Indians and some Sufis consider dance a type of prayer. Hindus chant mantras, burn fires, and meditate on specific Gods or Goddesses.[D] In Latin America, many tribes ingest psychoactive substances in order to experience the sacred. And, of course, Quakers listen in reverent silence.

In Africa, interactions with deity can occur in other ways. A Yoruba man or woman may become possessed by an *orisha*, one of the spirits in their pantheon, allowing others to then directly converse with the divine.

Divination ultimately refers to the divine inspiration we receive when we connect with the sacred within us or beyond us. For some of us, the divine will take the form of God (in monotheistic circles) or a particular God or Goddess. For others, the sacred may represent the spark of light within us or, alternatively, our higher or deeper selves—that part of us with a greater depth of insight than our ordinary ego-based personae. For still others, the holy will manifest as our ancestors, powerful dream figures, saints, angels, the elements (earth, air, fire, and water), nature, or as specific animal or plant guides. However the divine

dialogue with the sacred: address whatever deity or aspect of the sacred you feel will best answer your query.

WHERE — Anywhere

WHEN — Anytime

HOW — Sitting

TOOLS — A quiet place where you won't be interrupted

Two chairs, facing each other

discloses itself to you, trusting in its advice allows your mind to open to possibilities beyond the obvious. We dream big when we invite the divine to help us—which is just what science suggests we need for a eureka moment.[A]

This oracular method resembles prayer, since you dialogue with the divine during it—except you address the God, Goddess, saint, or animal spirit responsible for answering your question. For instance, if your query has to do with medical problems, you could ask for aid from the biblical doctor Saint Luke; Asklepios, the Greek God of medicine; the Celtic Bridget, Goddess of creativity and healing, and later a saint in the Catholic Church; or the frog, animal spirit of medicine and sensitivity within many Native American traditions. (For more information, see "Gods, Goddesses, Saints, and Power Animals," p. 226.)

This oracle involves my own adaptation of the "open chair technique," which helps encourage more holistic conversations with the divine. This psychological practice, developed by Gestalt therapists Fritz and Laura Perls, allows you to visualize the personification of the divine, sitting in the chair across from you. To begin, you simply represent your day-to-day self—the person with the oracular query. Once you have asked your question, you assume the role of your chosen divinity—the part of yourself that holds sacred wisdom—then converse back and forth. In this way, you become able to tune into the divine within.

STEPS

1. Formulate your question (p. 12).

2. Set two chairs opposite each other.

3. Ground and center (p. 15) while sitting on one of the chairs. Let your meditation create a space separate from your everyday life and a mind-set free of your ordinary, analytical thinking.

4. From this chair, imagine your chosen image of the divine in as much detail as possible. What is He wearing? How does She sit? How does He adorn himself? Does Her hair curl? Is His voice deep and strong or quiet and reassuring? What's unique about

Her? What mannerisms does He display? What other particulars bring Him or Her alive for you?

5. After envisioning this representation of the divine, acknowledge the process you are about to begin as your oracle.

6. State your divinatory question out loud while continuing to sit in the chair representing your everyday self. Gaze at the personification of the divine as if He or She were opposite you.

7. Once you have asked your question, switch chairs and assume the character of your chosen deity. Feel yourself inhabit His or Her body, clothes, and mannerisms.

8. When you have become the embodiment of your chosen aspect of the divine, answer the query you have just heard.

9. Switch chairs again, returning to your everyday self. Ask any follow-up questions you may have. (For more on formulating these questions, see chapter 1, p. 13.) Respond as the aspect of the divine you have chosen.

10. Continue the conversation until it ends naturally, asking follow-up questions as your day-to-day self and answering them as your chosen deity. Move between the chairs as you change roles.

11. Interpret your divination using free association (p. 18).

12. Thank the divine for your oracle.

CONTINUING THE JOURNEY

When you pose follow-up questions, be careful not to ask anything more than once. Doing so tends to negate the wisdom that has already come to you and, as a result, can shut down your intuition. Instead, simply ask your chosen divinity to tell you more. An open-ended request can facilitate further insight.

You can honor your divination by creating an "object of inner wisdom" (see p. 20) or by displaying a picture of your chosen deity. Remembering your inner wisdom on a regular basis will strengthen your connection with it.

DRUMMING
THE STEADY PULSE OF SPIRIT

› ADVANCED ‹

In the oldest cultures for which we have records—Sumer, Egypt, India, and Greece, among others—people played drums in order to connect with the divine. At Çatal Hüyük, one of the earliest cities in Anatolia, wall paintings portray a group dancing ecstatically and playing percussion instruments.[21] And in India, the sound produced by Hindu or Buddhist drumming represents the original *om*, the cosmic sound of the world being created.

Drumming is a powerful technique for inducing trance, a mental state that helps you connect more deeply with your wise guidance. Shamans from Asia and the Americas used drums—and still use them today—to transcend ordinary consciousness in order to travel to the spirit world for divinatory insight. Tom Keepers, a Cochiti drum maker, says, "To consult the drum, present your question to the drum and then play in a steady beat until it provides an answer. It's that simple and that profound." (For more information, visit "Drumming" in Resources, p. 226.)

Here's how it works. Drumming's ability to create an altered state of consciousness rests on its rhythmic quality. Regular rhythmic stimuli can synchronize the brain's waves to those same rhythms, inducing a deeply relaxing trance.

the steady pulse of spirit:
a steady beat on the drum pulls
the scattered pieces of your
mind into a vibrant state that's
open to your inner guidance.

WHERE — Anywhere

WHEN — Anytime

HOW — Sitting

TOOLS — A drum or a recording of drumming. (For information on where to purchase recordings, see "Drumming" in Resources, p. 226.)

A place where your drumming won't disturb others

A recent study by Barry Quinn, Ph.D., demonstrates that even a brief drumming session can double alpha brain wave activity.[22] As I've described in chapter 2, such alpha activity can lead to a sudden flash of intuition.

Whether you play the drums or just listen to them, the drumming experience can create alpha and theta waves in your brain, physiological changes that accompany trance (see chapter 1, p. 16) and spiritual experiences.[23] African drummers realized this long ago, calling the drumbeats they produced the "heartbeat of the earth," a name that Michael Harner, a cultural anthropologist and the founder of Foundation of Shamanic Studies, affirmed in his research. Harner explored drumming in many areas of the world and discovered that the rhythms of shamanic drumming are approximately the same as the base resonant frequency of the earth. This technique aligns you with the pulse of the drum for five to ten minutes, allowing you to enter an altered state of consciousness that can take you into your inner depths.

STEPS

1. Collect your tools.

2. Decide whether to produce the beat of your drum with your hands or a stick or to listen to a recording.

3. Formulate your question (p. 12).

4. Ground and center (p. 15). Let your meditation create a space separate from your everyday life and a mind-set free of your ordinary, analytical thinking.

5. State your question out loud.

6. If you're drumming, feel the drum against your body. Notice the sensation of your palms striking the drumhead. Experience the different sounds you produce and how your body responds to them. Feel the vibrations resonating through your hands into your arms and up into your torso. With each stroke, feel yourself becoming more in tune with the rhythm, synchronizing with the beat of the drum. Does your body begin to pulsate as well?

To sway back and forth, or undulate like the waves passing through it?

7. Whether you're drumming or not, let each pulse of the drum relax you into a profound meditative state. With each beat, feel yourself move deeper and deeper into a place of spiritual openness and inner knowing. Let the repetitive nature of the drumming mesmerize you. Stop thinking and connect with the pulse of the drum.

8. After ten minutes, stop the drumming and listen in the silence for your inner wisdom, if it hasn't already arrived.

9. Interpret the outcome. If necessary, use free association (p. 18) to help.

10. Thank your drum for your oracle.

CONTINUING THE JOURNEY

Any drum will work for this kind of divination, from a tambourine to a doumbek to bongos. If you're a very physical person, you might want to use a large kettledrum or frame drum that you can pound to your heart's content. But it really doesn't matter. Like some street musicians, you could even use a large plastic tub and a wooden spoon.

What does matter is keeping a rhythm that's fairly fast, approximately 180 beats per minute. This steady pulse will pull the bits and pieces of your mind into a resting place in the center of your being. Then, like chanting and dance, drumming can produce a feeling of vibrancy and vitality, even ecstasy. In this state, you're open to your deeper knowing and the nudgings of your inner voice. You stop thinking and connect with the pulse of the universe.

Some people may hear a voice within the drumbeats when they receive insight. Some may hear a sound that reminds them of a particular object, place, or time. Some may feel the heartbeat of Mother Earth followed by Her message. And most, I believe, will receive their divination after they have finished. But no matter when or how your intuition arrives, you'll be more receptive to your inner wisdom after less than fifteen minutes of drumming.

FIRE
WHISPERS OF FLAME

› ADVANCED ‹

Fire has been used since antiquity for divinations. The ancients called this oracular form *pyromancy*, from the Greek words for fire (*pyros*) and divination (*manteia*). Mesopotamian seers watched the smoke or ash of incense as it floated into the air or dropped from a burning stick.[24] And indigenous peoples all over the world also drew on fire for its oracular insights. In fact, in the mountains of Columbia, shamans still scrutinize the smoke from a cigarette or a torch to determine oracular questions.[c]

Of the four elements—earth, air, fire, and water—fire displays change most directly. In fact, many traditions call fire "the great transformer," because anything that burns changes radically as a result. In China, where each of these four elements have specific qualities associated with them, fire corresponds to the color red, to the direction south, to the sound of laughter, to the emotion of joy, and to the phoenix—a mythological bird that is destroyed by fire yet rises again triumphantly from its own ashes. As such, it's a powerful symbol of rebirth and renewal—a joyful, laughing phoenix rising from the fire!

In the West, too, we associate fire with the direction south. It represents willpower and passion, each of which are agents of change in their own right. A fire can also warm us in the winter or spark our imaginations if we watch its mesmerizing flames. And it's this final quality that influences us during divination.

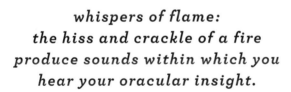

whispers of flame:
the hiss and crackle of a fire
produce sounds within which you
hear your oracular insight.

WHERE — **Near a fire**

WHEN — **Anytime**

HOW — **Sitting or standing**

TOOLS — **A fire**

The sounds of a fire can float you into a trance state (see chapter 1, p. 16) in which you can access your inner knowing, or they may remind you of certain words or phrases that answer your question. Watching your fire can also elicit the "flicker response"—a form of brain wave entrainment in which the brain's frequencies synchronize with the stimulus of the flames' oscillations. Instead of fluctuating at thirteen to thirty cycles per second (beta waves or alert consciousness), your brain slows down to eight to thirteen cycles per second—the range of alpha waves—where you enter an inward-focused state of serenity. If you've read chapter 2, you'll remember that alpha waves are a hallmark of creative insights, and that serenity is one of the positive emotions that's been shown to boost flashes of insight.[25] So, no matter how you engage with this divination, you're bound to tap into the wisdom of your deeper self.

STEPS

1. Formulate your question (p. 12).

2. Ground and center (p. 15). Let your meditation create a space separate from your everyday life and a mind-set free of your ordinary, analytical thinking.

3. Light a fire in a safe place (such as a campfire in a pit, a hearth fire, or a fire in a gas or wood stove).

4. Acknowledge your fire as your source of guidance.

5. State your question out loud and keep your eyes open.

6. Let yourself become mesmerized as you listen to the pops and hisses of your fire and watch it flicker and flash.

7. Let the sights and sounds of the fire lull you into a light trance (see chapter 1, p. 16).

8. As you float deeper into this altered state of consciousness, continue to watch the fire as it constantly changes yet remains

hypnotically the same. Listen to the crackles, pops, and hisses of the flames and notice if these sounds remind you of words. If there's a pop, does it emphasize something or awaken you to some insight you were entertaining? Do the small crackles sound like a conversation? If so, listen to what the flames are saying. Or, just let your mind drift for ten minutes. Either way, you will deepen into your inner counsel.

9. If you have yet to receive your oracle after ten minutes, close your eyes and listen to the fire for another five minutes.

10. Interpret your oracle, perhaps with the help of free association (p. 18).

11. Thank the fire for your oracle.

CONTINUING THE JOURNEY

It's always relaxing to sit by a fire. If you're like me, it may remind you of the tired-but-happy times you spent in front of a fire after walking, snowshoeing, skating, or cross-country skiing outside in winter. But being in the presence of a fire can do much more than calm or soothe. The warmth from the fire's heat is the first part of "warm anticipation," and the physical sensation of this kind of welcome heat invites you to enter a trance state in which you can contact your inner knowing. (See chapter 1, p. 17, for more about warmly anticipating your oracle.) Plus, our brains are hypersensitive to color and motion as well as pattern, so fires mesmerize us easily. This makes fire a powerful tool for contacting your inner wisdom.

In this kind of auditory oracle, it's possible to hear words forming between the snaps, crackles, and pops of the fire. And sometimes, the rhythm of the sounds resembles the pattern of sentences that shape themselves in your mind. Of course, you might also simply enter trance and discover your guidance that way. But in either case, you'll come to understand something that has eluded you until then.

GUIDED MEDITATION
YOUR WISE FRIEND'S COUNSEL

› BASIC ‹

Guided meditation might seem to be a modern technique, but it's actually based on ancient shamanic practices. Paleolithic cave paintings indicate that these methods date back to our earliest ancestors. Like guided meditation, such shamanic techniques involve visions in which the seer interacts with his or her spirit guides.

Within modern psychology, guided meditation also has a history. During his early years, Sigmund Freud used a "concentration technique" that involved contemplating evocative scenes. Carl Jung, after his break with Freud, introduced "active imagination," a psychological method that allowed his patients to interact and talk with significant symbols. Influenced by Freud and Jung, Robert Desoille created "directed waking dream" therapy in the 1930s and 1940s, and Hanscarl Leuner began "guided affective imagery" in the 1960s.[26] Similar to dream narratives, today's guided meditations refer to a process in which people close their eyes, relax, and then follow a script (either recorded or live) that engages their imagination in order to help them with a specific issue or goal.

your wise friend's counsel:
imagine walking through a beautiful
landscape to meet a wise being
who tells you what you need to know.

WHERE — Anywhere private

WHEN — Anytime

HOW — Sitting or lying down

TOOLS — A quiet place where you won't be interrupted

A friend to read the guided meditation (steps 5–19), or a recording of it being read

Paper and pen to write down your experience

Whether you ask a friend to read this guided meditation or record it for yourself, be sure to speak slowly and allow long pauses of between fifteen and thirty seconds where they're indicated.

STEPS

1. Collect your tools.

2. Find a quiet place where you won't be interrupted.

3. Formulate your question (p. 12).

4. Ground and center (p. 15). Let your meditation create a space separate from your everyday life and a mind-set free of your ordinary, analytical thinking.

5. Imagine that you are in one of your favorite places—either a place you know and love well or someplace you have always wanted to visit. You feel comfortable and expansive in this spot, which embraces you with its vibrant beauty.

6. Look around you. What do you see? (Pause.) What do you hear? (Longer pause.) Feel the energy of this place: how it revitalizes you, how it relaxes you. (Longer pause.) Breathe deeply and enjoy this place of sacred wisdom. Open your awareness to the colors, fragrances, and sounds you find here. (Longer pause.)

7. Wander around this landscape, looking and touching, listening and smelling, until you come to a comfortable place to sit. (Longer pause.) Here, you can relax and wait for the enlightened being who will answer your question. You're in no hurry. Wait until a wise one joins you. (Pause.)

8. After a while you hear something—a rustling, a door opening, a movement of some kind. Soon you realize that it's the sound of someone entering this extraordinary and wonderful place. You look up and see your friendly guide. (Short pause.) Is it someone you know and love? Or someone you've always longed to meet? (Short pause.) Does this being surprise you in some way? (Longer pause.)

9. Look into the knowing, loving eyes of this person or animal. Notice their wisdom. (Longer pause.)

10. You may wish to walk around this place and converse with the wise one who has joined you. Or you may want to sit in some snug corner, holding hands and communing with each other. Whatever you wish, first greet your guide and then ask him or her your question. (Pause.)

11. Your friend lovingly tells you what you need to know. (Very long pause.)

12. You are grateful for your wise friend's guidance, and thank him or her. (Pause.)

13. When you're finished, ask this wise one if there's anything else you need to hear? (Long pause.)

14. Before your loving friend departs, ask your guide if there is a gift for you. (Long pause.)

15. Notice what this enlightened being has given to you. Take it into your hands, if appropriate. What does it look like? (Pause.) Does it make any sound? (Pause.) Does it have a scent? (Pause.) What does it feel like? (Pause.)

16. Ask your friend what power this gift holds for you and where you should carry it. (Longer pause.)

17. You are very grateful for the gift you have received and thank your guide once again. (Pause.)

18. Now it is time to leave. Your enlightened friend tells you that you can return at any time so that he or she can answer your questions, and then says good-bye and turns to leave. You take one last look at your favorite place and then begin slowly to return to your present reality, remembering everything that has happened, especially the answer to your question and the gift you have received. (Pause.)

19. When you feel ready, slowly come back to your day-to-day reality by opening your eyes.

20. Record your guided meditation. When you feel ready, begin to explore its meaning. If you don't immediately understand it, use free association (p. 18) to discover its implications.

21. Thank your wise friend for your oracle.

CONTINUING THE JOURNEY

Hearing an inner voice of wisdom has been a form of spiritual guidance from ancient times. This makes sense, since scientific research is now speculating that the same neural pathways (mirror neurons) fire in the brain whether you perform an action or simply imagine it. So, if you speak to a wise guide in your mind, it's almost the same as talking to this "guru" in person. One way to honor your friend's guidance is to create an image of the gift you were given as an "object of inner wisdom" (see p. 20 for more on objects of inner wisdom) and to display it where you will see it often.

Remember that a guided meditation like the one I've shared here may not work for everyone the first time. Becoming acquainted with your sacred inner landscape and getting comfortable with its sights and sounds may be a first step toward welcoming a wise guide. If no one comes to you the first time you try this meditation, don't worry: This may change in the future. Besides, simply entering into the state of a guided meditation has many benefits, including relaxation, which is key to fostering insight.

INTUITION
LISTENING WITH INNER EARS

› ADVANCED ‹

Seers and psychics have used their intuition to help others since the beginning of time. Perhaps the most famous seer was the Pythia of Delphi, a priestess who delivered oracles from her shrine in ancient Greece. During biblical times, visionaries like Joseph interpreted dreams for their kings. And ancient Islamic geomancers read sand patterns as a means of understanding the universe. In fact, psychic adepts have used their intuition in every culture: Diné (Navaho) stargazers, Nepali shamanic healers called *Jankri*, Euahlalyi diviners in northeastern Australia, and Hispanic *curanderas* (folk healers) are just a few examples.[C]

Listening with Inner Ears invites seekers to descend deep within to hear the still, small voice of their intuitive wisdom. Scientific experiments have shown that this kind of internal focus minimizes the distractions that can block a sudden insight from arising.[A]

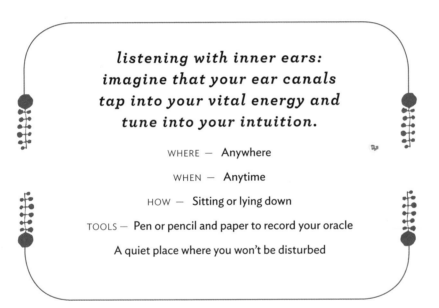

listening with inner ears:
imagine that your ear canals
tap into your vital energy and
tune into your intuition.

WHERE — Anywhere

WHEN — Anytime

HOW — Sitting or lying down

TOOLS — Pen or pencil and paper to record your oracle

A quiet place where you won't be disturbed

I created Listening with Inner Ears to directly access your inner voice. It's a method of auditory divining that allows you to move, step-by-step, into the inner chamber where your oracular wisdom resides.

As quantum physicists, mystics, and psychics of all types remind us, our universe is made up of energy that constantly moves and changes. Just like the energy around us, human beings ebb and flow. And, like the cosmos, we literally embody a dynamic web of energy patterns that have been described by many cultures in terms of the vital life force of *prana* (Hinduism), the astral light

(Kabbalistic Judaism), or *qi* (Taoism), to name a few. In this technique, you will hear your inner knowing within the energetic field of your own qi—the vital energy of your life force.

Although qi is energy, if you listen carefully, you will hear that it also has a "voice." Can energy speak and impart information? Yes: In fact, in many energy medicine practices, energy *is* information.

STEPS

1. Collect your tools.

2. Find a quiet place where you won't be disturbed.

3. Formulate your question (p. 12).

4. Ground and center (p. 15). Let your meditation create a space separate from your everyday life and a mind-set free of your ordinary, analytical thinking.

5. Close your eyes and imagine that your ear canals extend inward, so that you can hear the vital energy (qi) flowing through your body. Imagine that these tubes, which run from your outer ear into your middle ear, are growing longer and developing extra-sensitive nerve fibers that can detect this special sound.

6. Listen carefully and notice how your inner hearing begins to attune itself to the energetic pulsation of your qi, picking up on your inner frequency. It may sound like a low hum—the primordial song of the universe—running along your spine and throughout your torso and limbs. It may sound like a hive of bees or the quiver of a violin string in the wind.

7. Now take a few deep, relaxing breaths. Become as calm and peaceful as possible.

8. With each breath, turn up the volume of your inner wisdom. Your inner ears are becoming more and more sensitive to the sounds within and more able to hear what your intuition has to say.

9. With the next few purifying breaths, imagine that your auditory perception is becoming even sharper, as if you were tuning a dial on your inner radio. As you harken more attentively, your inner signals begin to sound more like words.

10. When you feel ready, state your question silently or out loud.

11. If it helps, envision a wise figure talking to you on your wavelength—a person who is responding to your question.

12. Listen for your oracular answer.

13. Once you've heard what you need to know, thank your inner depths for your oracle.

14. Now let the volume of your intuition decrease. Let your inner hearing fade as you return your ear canals to their usual length.

15. Take a few moments to notice what your outer ears hear and then return to your everyday consciousness and open your eyes.

16. Interpret your divination, perhaps using free association (p. 18).

17. Thank your inner wisdom once again for your oracle.

CONTINUING THE JOURNEY

People often think of intuition as a hunch, an impression, or a feeling of certainty that they can't explain logically. For our purposes, "intuition" means a direct channel to your inner wisdom. (After all, energy medicine specialists believe that the body literally holds inner wisdom: cellular memory, for instance, is the concept that individual cells can contain stored memories.) Your inner wisdom can materialize as inner vision, an inner voice of insight, or an inner feeling of affirmation; in this case, the technique utilizes the auditory sense.

When you undertake an auditory divination, what you hear will sometimes take the form of words or a noise perceived by your "outer" ears and sometimes as an "inner" voice or sound. Here, it's the latter: This oracle asks you to listen to the mysterious internal voice that knows you better than you know yourself. Hearing your inner voice is an auditory ability you can develop, just as you can improve your visual or kinesthetic skills for divination.

LEAVES
RUSTLING MESSAGES

› ADVANCED ‹

Leaves have supported human lives since the very beginnings of our species. They have fed us, healed us, and quenched our thirst. They have dyed our clothing, added spice to our food, and beautified our gardens. So it's no surprise that leaves have had great significance in our medicine, handicrafts, cooking, and culture. But most significantly, leaves transform the sun's energy, providing us with oxygen to breathe. Without the life-sustaining process of photosynthesis that leaves provide, life on earth wouldn't exist as it does today.

As a result of their importance to human life, leaves have played an active role in divination since ancient times. In classical Greece, diviners received oracles from Zeus by listening to the oak leaves at his shrine in Dodona.[27] The most famous ancient Greek seer, the Sybil of Cumae, supposedly left her prophecies written on leaves at the mouth of her cave.[G] And in the Hebrew Bible, King David waited for a sign from God to begin an attack on the Philistines. When he heard the sound of marching in the topmost leaves of a nearby mulberry tree, he interpreted this as the signal to march against his enemy.[28]

Similarly, traditional American Indians receive divinations by hearing the voices of their ancestors in the leaves of trees, bushes, and flowers.[29] Ashanti diviners in Africa are also trained to listen to the voices of the trees around them

rustling messages:
within the rustles, scratches,
creaks, and rasps of the leaves on
your chosen tree or bush, you listen
to the voice of your inner wisdom.

WHERE — A natural area

WHEN — Anytime

HOW — Sitting or standing

TOOLS — A park, backyard, or wilderness area

Wind, from gentle breezes to strong gusts

A tree(s) or other plant(s)

in their oracles.[30] And in Albania, women who perform divinations throw a special leaf into their fires and hear an oracle in the sounds it makes as it burns.[C]

The swish and sigh of leaves rustling in the wind creates a kind of "white noise," a wide-spectrum sound that mimics many people whispering together. Scientists have now shown that the sensory restriction such noises produce facilitates eureka experiences.[A] It's easier to hear these noises in the fall when the leaves are dry and brittle: If you want to undertake this divination method during other months, find a large tree or shrub in a quiet place, away from other noises that might distract you.

STEPS

1. On a windy day, find a natural area (park, woodland, beach, backyard, garden, or wilderness) that is relatively undisturbed by noises other than the rustling leaves in the tree, bush, or grasses you have chosen. Acknowledge this place as your source of guidance.

2. Formulate your question (p. 12).

3. Ground and center (p. 15). Let your meditation create a space separate from your everyday life and a mind-set free of your ordinary, analytical thinking.

4. State your question out loud.

5. Close your eyes and listen to the sound of the wind as it whispers through the leaves. Let the noises you hear mesmerize you into a light trance (see chapter 1, p. 16).

6. Tune into the rustle, scratch, creak, and rasp of the leaves. Do they remind you of anything? Do their sounds call up an experience or a thought for you? Let these noises dance around the edges of your mind, tugging you toward greater understanding.

7. Do the swish and sigh of the leaves have a rhythm? Does their regular pattern sound like a conversation to you? Eavesdrop. Does a crack become a word? Does a creak evoke a phrase? Between the noises, do you hear the internal voice of your own intuitive knowledge?

8. Let the sounds sweep by your ears and notice what you hear around you or in your mind.

9. If you have not received oracular guidance after ten minutes, meditate for five more minutes.

10. Restate your question and listen for a minute more.

11. Interpret your oracle, perhaps with the help of free association (p. 18).

12. Thank the leaves for your oracle.

CONTINUING THE JOURNEY

Your oracle may come in the form of words from your inner depths, external sounds that act as an insight trigger, or as sounds that mirror the emotional pattern of your answer. You may be unconsciously mulling over something when a sharp snap calls attention to it, and you become aware of that thought. Or, if you're like me, you might begin to hear phrases or words that echo the sounds of the leaves. Whichever the case, your divination will allow you to tap into the source of your intuitive knowledge concerning your query.

After you've recorded your oracle, you could also create an "object of inner wisdom" using your intuitive knowledge as a springboard. Did your divination have a storyline? Write a tale that begins with this narrative. Were the words whispered by the leaves lyrical in some way? Write a poem to evoke their insight. And when you're finished, leave your writing out where you can see it and remember the insightful counsel of your divination.

PEOPLE
A STRANGER GIVES YOU DIRECTION

› BASIC ‹

As human beings, we're fascinated with one another, and the ancients found other people just as captivating as we do today, even consulting them as oracles. One of the most famous oracles was the seer at Delphi, whom Greeks visited for divination. But Greeks and Romans also sought divinatory insight from ordinary citizens, people who were totally unaware of their function as oracles. One way of soliciting such guidance was to listen to chance snippets of conversation, or to determine that the next person who spoke would offer the answer to a divinatory question. These omens were known as *cledons* (pronounced "clay-dons") and were highly prized communications from the Gods, especially if delivered by a child.

a stranger gives you direction: in a public place, ask your question silently or under your breath and then wait for a stranger to answer it.

WHERE — In a public place

WHEN — When people gather

HOW — Sitting, standing, or walking

TOOLS — A well-populated street, shopping center, office building, restaurant, etc.

The **People** oracle consists of random words or phrases, often heard out of context, that provide oracular advice. You can purposefully elicit this type of divination by going to a public place. Visiting a shopping mall or busy street has the added benefit of changing your context, which, according to the most recent research, increases the odds of encountering an insight trigger.[A]

STEPS

1. Formulate your question (p. 12).

2. Determine where you will perform your oracle.

3. Ground and center at your chosen location (p. 15). Let your meditation create a space separate from your everyday life and a mind-set free of your ordinary, analytical thinking.

4. When the time feels right, ask your question silently or under your breath.

5. Listen for the next words you hear. They may come from a nearby person or jump out at you from a crowd in the distance. What you hear might shock you, quietly enlighten you, or require further thought to figure out. But the first words you hear will answer your question.

6. Interpret your oracle, perhaps with free association (p. 18).

7. Thank the cledon for your oracle.

CONTINUING THE JOURNEY

A **People** divination can offer amazing advice when you least expect it. You'll find that your answer often comes as soon as someone approaches close enough for you to hear, although sometimes one voice may seem to jump out at you from a nearby group or you might catch a random snatch of conversation while people walk by. It's important to listen carefully to the very first words you hear, because they hold a wisdom that will often boggle your mind with its accuracy.

The timing of your question is a significant factor in this divination. Trust your intuition and wait until you feel the urge to state it, either silently or under your breath. Sometimes you'll feel an impulse to ask your question immediately. Other times, it may feel right to pause for a while. It's amazing that complete strangers will answer your oracular question without the smallest inkling that you've even overheard them.

REPEATED CUES

BRAINSTORMING NEW PERSPECTIVES

› BASIC ‹

One of the best ways to tap into your intuition involves "lateral thinking." This term, coined by psychologist Edward de Bono in his 1967 book *New Think: The Use of Lateral Thinking*, describes an indirect and creative approach to solving problems. Some people call this "thinking outside the box." Lateral thinking uses nontraditional reasoning and unconventional logic to generate new perspectives on an issue. According to de Bono, "lateral thinking is for changing concepts and perceptions." It's not about rearranging what we already know, but about changing the way we perceive a given situation so we can reach new insights.

Since most of de Bono's techniques have circulated widely in North America, many people have learned about them in contexts other than creativity studies and problem solving. When I read about his "idea-generating tools," I was amazed to discover that several of the divination methods I had devised or adapted could be seen as special cases of his methods. For instance, **Books** turns out to be an example of his "random entry idea generating tool," while **Balloon Diagrams** represents his "concept fan idea generating tool." **Repeated Cues** resembles his "challenge idea generating tool," in which someone repeatedly asks "Why?" about a problem until a new idea emerges. However, Repeated Cues involves answering three prompts. All of these techniques entail insight triggers, which—as science has proven—work best when the brain is in an expansive, defocused state.[31] So make sure you ground and center before you use this technique.

brainstorming new perspectives: responding to repeated cues, you hear yourself uttering new insights about your issue.

WHERE — **Anywhere**

WHEN — **Anytime**

HOW — **Sitting, standing, or lying down**

TOOLS — **A friend to give you cues**

A recording device (optional)

A pencil and paper

I learned this powerful form of gathering ideas in a class about the chakras taught by author Ingrid Dilley, creator of the Renewing Life Program, and nurse practitioner Marcia Pollock. My Buddhist friends use a similar process called "inquiry" and tell me that it originated within the Diamond Approach, created by A.H. Almaas, whose teaching combines ancient spiritual traditions with modern depth psychology to open up spiritual truths.

STEPS

1. Formulate your question (p. 12).

2. Arrange for a friend to help you and provide him or her with note-taking materials.

3. Ground and center (p. 15). Let your meditation create a space separate from your everyday life and a mind-set free of your ordinary, analytical thinking.

4. State your question out loud.

5. Once you've stated your question, your friend prompts you by saying **"I'm afraid..."** You respond with whatever comes immediately to mind. Your friend writes down your response while giving you the same cue: "I'm afraid." Your friend continues to prompt you with this cue for five minutes, recording your replies. It's important for the friend to cue you rapidly so you don't have time to mull over your answer.

6. Then your friend prompts you with the second cue: **"I would like..."** Once again, you respond with whatever comes to mind. Your friend records what you say while simultaneously giving you the same cue. Your friend continues to prompt you with this cue for five minutes, eliciting and recording rapid replies.

7. Then your friend prompts you by saying, "**I choose...**" You reply with whatever comes to mind. Your friend records what you say while simultaneously giving you the same cue. Your friend continues to prompt you with this cue for five minutes, eliciting and recording rapid replies.

8. Interpret the results. Look over your answers and see what strikes you. If necessary, use free association (p. 18).

9. Thank your unconscious for your oracle.

CONTINUING THE JOURNEY

Speed facilitates this divination. When a friend prompts you rapidly and you answer in kind, you'll often receive ingenious ideas or suggestions. If your friend can manage it, it's best for him or her to provide the next cue while writing down your previous answer. If this is impossible, use a recording device so that your friend can concentrate on rapid-fire questions and answers. He or she can speed up your response time by repeating the cue when you hesitate or balk.

Allowing yourself to stray from your divinatory question—if that's what your mind wants to do—will also help you succeed with this oracular method. When you seem to wander away from the subject, your mental path often brings you closer to an answer.

It's very important to give yourself the full five minutes for each of the cues, even if you feel your divinatory question has already been answered. That's because your last responses may give you a deeper or broader picture of both your situation and its possible resolutions.

If you get stuck while using **Repeated Cues** and feel you've only discovered what you already know, you may have been answering too slowly. You may also have been unable or unwilling to let go of conscious control. When this happens, try moving your oracular question to the back burner of your mind. I tried this recently, and within an hour, I realized what had blocked me—and, as a consequence, what I needed to do about my query. It's amazing what your unconscious will tell you if it's given enough time.

SOUNDS
ECHOES OF YOUR SPIRIT

› BASIC ‹

The song "Breaths," by the women's a cappella group Sweet Honey in the Rock, exhorts us to "listen more often to things than to beings," calling listeners to hear voices in the crackling fire, the flowing waters, the "rustling trees," the "crying grass," and even among people in a crowd. Indigenous cultures have always taken this counsel seriously. A Lingít (Tlingit) girl living in northwest Canada, for instance, might listen to the ear bone from a salmon to discover which man she should marry. The Onandowaga (Senecas) tuned into sounds made by a variety of plants and animals, among them birds, mammals, and trees. The noises that the wind produces in trees provided oracular advice for the ancient Israelites as well as the Ashanti tribe in Africa. And Diné (Navajo) diviners listened to the wind itself as it whistled across their arid countryside.[C]

In Europe, the ancient Greeks called this type of sound divination *alveromancy*. Other ancient Europeans also used such oracles, among them the Celtic Scots. An early Scottish shaman would perform a ritual called *taghairm* that involved the noises of a waterfall: The seer would spend the night discovering the answer to a pressing question by listening to the roar of the water.[C] If as a child you listened to seashells to "hear the ocean roar," you might find it interesting that this activity probably began as a type of **Sounds** divination as well.[H]

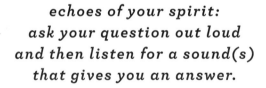

echoes of your spirit:
ask your question out loud
and then listen for a sound(s)
that gives you an answer.

WHERE — **Anywhere**

WHEN — **Anytime**

HOW — **Sitting, standing, or lying down**

TOOLS — **None**

Taking a break from your problem and performing an **Echoes of Your Spirit** divination makes it possible to receive an "insight trigger" for understanding the quandary you're in. As science has recently shown, insight triggers can loosen your analytic mind-set when it's stuck on obvious answers and can open you to less immediately apparent possibilities.[^]

You can perform Echoes of Your Spirit anywhere, but you will hear different sounds depending on the location you choose. If you select a natural site, you may need to interpret a bird's song, the wind's rustle, or an animal's cry. If you're inside your own home, the sound(s) you notice may be the telephone ringing, someone's voice, or noises from outdoors muffled by the glass in your windows.

No matter where you decide to carry out your oracle, your interpretive object remains the same: to freely associate with the sound you've heard. If you hear a dog bark, does that mean someone's angry? Or if you notice your spouse's voice in the next room, does that mean that he or she might be able to help you with your issue? If someone turns on the faucet, does the running water imply that something about your issue is being washed away? These are the types of questions you need to ask yourself.

If you're an auditory person, like me, you may find sound oracles very satisfying. While listening in the woods, on the beach, or in a park, you might find yourself transported into the realm of mystery. As a result, sometimes the particular divination you're performing will take a backseat to the magic that enters your life when you truly open your ears.

STEPS

1. Decide where you will perform your divination.

2. Formulate your question (p. 12).

3. Ground and center (p. 15). Let your meditation create a space separate from your everyday life and a mind-set free of your ordinary, analytical thinking.

4. Ask your question out loud.

5. Listen for the first sound(s) that attracts your attention. You may have to listen for up to two to three minutes or until you hear a response to your query.

6. If your guidance hasn't arrived after three minutes, meditate silently for a few minutes. Then, restate your question and listen for at least one more minute.

7. Interpret your oracle, perhaps with the help of free association (p. 18).

8. Thank the sound(s) for your oracle.

CONTINUING THE JOURNEY

Here's a personal example of how this technique can work. While writing this entry, I had a funny experience that demonstrates the kind of awareness you need to develop in order to become sensitive to the sounds in your environment. I had decided to do an **Echoes of Your Spirit** oracle, asking the question, "Are there any other kinds of divinations that I should include in *The World Is Your Oracle?*"

While grounding and centering, my mother-in-law telephoned, stopping my divination before it had begun. Since I had already been interrupted, I decided to take a bathroom break, during which I noticed that the noise the toilet roll seemed to make as I unwound it sounded a lot like the word "No." I also heard one of my neighbor's doors slam shut, its thud reverberating with the "No" I had already heard. But, being stubborn, I went back to my easy chair to finish grounding and centering, and while doing this, the timer I had set—to get me up and moving after a half hour of being sedentary—went off. Clearly it was telling me to stop what I was doing. After the timer buzzed, I finally listened to the accumulated sounds that had repeated "Stop" and "No" a total of four times. It took me a while, but I realized that I didn't need any additional divination methods for this book.

TONING

SOUNDS FROM YOUR DEPTHS

› ADVANCED ‹

Like warm-up exercises for improvisatory acting, toning involves listening to your creative impulses and then expressing them with your voice. This free-form vocalization is unlike other types of singing, since it has no given structure, melody, lyrics, or rhythm. Instead, you create it as you go along.

I've adapted this modern form of improvising as an oracular method because it has proven to be a powerful tool in my own life. Undertaking a **Toning** divination allows you to hear your emotions surrounding your query. Among other purposes, this technique can release pent-up feelings, balance your emotional landscape, help you accept certain situations, or lead to new understandings of your circumstances. And when you get your emotions moving, you clear unconscious blocks to their awareness.

For all these reasons, Toning embraces the whole range of vocal expression—from quiet to noisy, slow to fast, and from the sublime to the strident. In fact, this vocal "stream of consciousness" covers the gamut of noisemaking, from rhythmic beats to drawn-out notes, from lyrical melodies to animal calls, from the sweet caress of humming to the raucous noise of screaming, and from seemingly random sounds to words or even phrases—although, in my experience, words are few and far between. The impulse for sound making comes from a more primal part of the psyche than the parts of the brain that control speech.

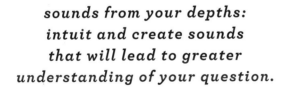

sounds from your depths:
intuit and create sounds
that will lead to greater
understanding of your question.

WHERE — A quiet place

WHEN — Anytime

HOW — Sitting or standing

TOOLS — A place where you won't disturb anyone and won't be interrupted

If you've never toned, loosen up by mimicking animal or bird noises—just as you did as a child—or make any sounds that appeal to you. You can also let your voice slide from the lowest note you can sing to the highest and then back again.

Toning often involves staying with the sounds and emotions that emerge in order to move through them. Thus, it can be profoundly cathartic whether or not you release negative emotions. Listening to your intuition and making the sounds it desires will ultimately lead to a clearer understanding of your divinatory question.

STEPS

1. Find a place where you won't be interrupted while toning.

2. Formulate your question (p. 12).

3. Ground and center (p. 15). Let your meditation create a space separate from your everyday life and a mind-set free of your ordinary, analytical thinking.

4. State your question out loud.

5. Warm up your voice in whatever way feels good to you.

6. Take three deep breaths, exaggerating the last. Continue this until your breathing noises transform or you begin to hear other sounds that you want to make. Explore these noises, tones, vowel sounds, and vocalizations. Listen into your depths and let the sounds of your issue move through your voice and body.

7. Tone for five minutes or so. Expressing what you feel about your issue might morph into something else. Or you may find yourself "singing a different tune" than you expected.

8. Listen for your guidance in the stillness that follows your toning.

9. Interpret the outcome, possibly with free association, p. 18, or the "Continuing the Journey" guidelines.

10. Thank the sounds you made for their wisdom.

CONTINUING THE JOURNEY

This technique can help auditory diviners understand a confusing situation better than almost any other method and can also have a healing effect. According to Mitchell L. Gaynor, M.D., author of *The Healing Power of Sound*, "sound—which has vibratory effects on cells and organs, emotional effects on the brain, and which taps a spiritual dimension as yet undefined—is the next frontier in holistic healing."

The first few seconds of toning usually help you let go of physical stresses. After a short while, your vocalizations begin to tap into the primary emotion(s) of your issue and often unconsciously voice your mood(s) about it. If you let these sounds deepen, they will morph into another "feeling tone," giving you an indication of the emotional layers of your question. Depending on your query, there may be movement from one emotion to another—and, as a result, from one sound to another.

In interpreting your experience, it's useful to ask yourself what you felt as you toned. Some questions that might help you include the following:

- What did your issue sound like? Did you make frustrated noises? Or sigh over and over, perhaps in resignation? Scream with fear or pain? Was it hard for you to raise your voice? Did you hiss? Growl?

- What tonal qualities did you use? Deep and rich? Thin and colorless, like a sad child? Loud and strident? Muffled or muted? Flat and lifeless? Gentle and comforting? Hollow or low?

- Which urges did you translate into sound? Happiness? Resignation? Anger? Pain? Sorrow? Fear? Confusion?

- Did you make animal noises? Which ones? What does that tell you about your issue? (See "Associations with Common North American Animals," p. 234, for ideas about their meanings.)

- How fast or slow did you vocalize? How did this pace affect your mood? Did it move to another emotional dimension?

- Did you start to sing a song? If so, what were its lyrics? What kind of melody did it have? Was it melancholy? Upbeat? A dance? Something hymnlike? Or jazzy? Suspenseful? A lullaby?

- What rhythms did you use? Short, sharp beats, indicating energy? Pulsing sounds? Long, drawn-out notes? A waltz? A march?

WATER

RIPPLES OF TRUTH

› ADVANCED ‹

Water makes up one of the four major elements in many spiritual traditions. In China, it corresponds to the color black, to the direction north, to the tortoise, to the hours of the night, to the sense of listening, and to the relation of friendship. Chinese seers also associate water with the moon, just as we do in the West. Western spiritual traditions link water primarily with emotion, especially those feelings that bring tears to your eyes, such as joy, sorrow, frustration, and grief. Western culture also views water as the element of intuition, dreams, and receptivity. Water implies purification as well, and in our part of the world, we associate it with the direction west. Decks of playing cards also relate it to the suit of hearts, reinforcing its tie to the emotions.

From these descriptions of water's mystical connotations, it's not surprising that it has figured prominently in divination. The ancients called these oracular methods *hydromancy*, from the Greek *hydör*, meaning "water," and *manteia*, meaning "divination." Herodotus records that the Pythia sometimes received her inspiration by drinking waters from the Cassotis Spring at Delphi.[32] And both Virgil and Cicero tell us that the priestesses at Dodona sometimes listened to the water's murmurs in the sacred fountain as well as the sacred oak tree's whispering.[33]

Today, people from a number of cultures still use water for oracular purposes. In the Czech Republic, Denmark, and Malta, men and women read the shapes formed by molten lead as it's poured into a water-filled bowl. In Tibet, the head of the household performs a similar oracle as a New Year's divination, using

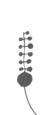

ripples of truth: the sound of an ocean, stream, or lake will float information forward in your mind.

WHERE — **Near water**

WHEN — **Anytime**

HOW — **Sitting or standing**

TOOLS — **A body of water or your own faucet**

butter instead of lead. And on the Marquesan Islands in the Pacific, seers fill taro leaves with water and gaze into them for oracular insight.[c]

A gurgling stream, a lake lapping gently on the shore, ocean waves crashing on a beach, or even water splashing from your shower or kitchen or bathtub faucet all create sounds that will answer oracular questions. The hypnotic quality of water's movement combined with the "white noise" of its sound allows a person to quickly enter a light trance state (see chapter 1, p. 16) and pick out a voice(s) among the splash and trickle that will soon give guidance. Such an altered state of consciousness is characterized by alpha waves, which have been shown to create a bridge between your conscious and your unconscious mind.[34]

STEPS

1. Formulate your question (p. 12).

2. Decide on the body of water you wish to use as your divination tool. Acknowledge it as your source of guidance.

3. Ground and center near this body of water (p. 15). Let your meditation create a space separate from your everyday life and a mind-set free of your ordinary, analytical thinking.

4. State your question out loud.

5. Listen to the movement of the water until you hear an answer to your question. Let its noises mesmerize you into a light trance (see chapter 1, p. 16). Notice the water's rhythms as it rushes and murmurs. Does it sound like a phrase or a sentence to you? Does a splash become a word in your mind? Does the crash of a wave become an exclamation point? If you're inside, does the "splat" on the bottom of your sink indicate the end of a sentence? Do the currents and sprays remind you of something that slipped your mind until now? Listen to the melody the water sings. Let it sing an answer to your question.

6. If you have not received oracular guidance after ten minutes, meditate in silence for five more minutes.

7. Restate your question and listen for a minute more.

8. Interpret your oracle, perhaps with the help of free association (p. 18).

9. Thank the water for your oracle.

CONTINUING THE JOURNEY

Remember that the stream nearest you may flow from your bathroom or kitchen faucet. When you resort to your kitchen sink for this type of divination, recall Thich Nhat Hanh, the famous Vietnamese Buddhist monk who supposedly loved washing dishes, because it was an easy way to be in the present moment. In fact, you could perform this type of oracle while washing your own dishes.

Personally, this is my favorite type of oracle and probably one of my major reasons for living next to a lake. I often walk down to the edge of the water to ask the waves for advice if something is puzzling me. After a few moments, I hear the murmuring or splashing water answer my question. When I listen to the lake, it seems to speak in an almost human voice that always offers insight into my problems. But I'm not only listening to the waves; I'm also experiencing a more interconnected set of relationships. My lifelong love of water, my feeling of root-edness on Lake Mendota, my search for guidance, my meditative stillness, *plus* the murmur of the waves allow me to tap into the wisdom available to me at that moment. The same can be true for you when you perform this kind of divination.

5

KINESTHETIC

TECHNIQUES

THE CONCEPT OF "BODYMIND" has gained a lot of traction in the last few decades. Recognizing that the human mind and body are a single integrated unit has led to alternative approaches in medicine—for instance, meditating to enhance physical health—and has made us aware that our bodies are repositories of memories, feelings, and experiences that are not always accessible to our conscious minds.

That's where kinesthetic divinations come in. Such oracles allow you to access your physical wisdom about concerns that might otherwise escape your conscious scrutiny. Some of the divination techniques gathered here encourage you to pay attention to your "vibes" or "gut feelings"—for example, by following your hands and feet or connecting with your body's signals. Others allow you to act out your concern, by creating a sculpture or doodling, for instance. Still others facilitate a trance state—brought on by dancing ecstatically or meditating—as a gateway to inner wisdom.

BODY SENSE

GETTING IN TOUCH

› BASIC ‹

In Western culture, we often ignore the body and its ways of knowing. But among indigenous peoples, physically felt oracles provide a rich source of insight. Shamans from the mountains of Colombia look for unusual sensations in their *own* bodies to give them information about their patients. In North America, the Apache Indians take note of involuntary tremors as indications of either positive or negative events to come.[c] And with the advent of holistic medicine in the West, some practitioners—Louise Hay, for example—have come to view physical symptoms as embodied metaphors for emotional or psychological issues. As a result, Westerners are beginning to recognize that our bodies contain rich insights if we pay attention to them.

getting in touch: follow a guided meditation to tap into your body's wisdom.

WHERE — **Anywhere private**

WHEN — **Anytime**

HOW — **Sitting or lying down**

TOOLS — **A friend to read the guided meditation (steps 4–19) or a recording of it**

A pencil and paper to record to your divination experience

Body sense is a term indicating a physical sensation that corresponds to some thought or emotion that has yet to be understood or expressed. I created **Getting in Touch** as a means of connecting—literally—with your body's signals, using your "intuitive feel" about an issue to understand it more fully.[35] It's important to read this guided meditation slowly and with pauses of between fifteen and thirty seconds.

STEPS

1. Collect your tools.

2. Formulate your question (p. 12).

3. Ground and center (p. 15). Let your meditation create a space separate from your everyday life and a mind-set free of your ordinary, analytical thinking.

4. Close your eyes and take at least three relaxing breaths.

5. Now mentally move through your body, noticing where you feel most comfortable, most centered, most yourself. Scan your entire body, looking for the place you feel most physically rooted, most connected to yourself: from your head (Pause), down through your neck (Pause), to your torso and all your internal organs (Pause), down your arms (Pause), then on to your pelvis (Pause), down your legs (Pause), to your feet (Pause), and finally to your toes. (Long pause.) Once you've found it, you'll know this is the place where you feel most deeply connected to your body and to yourself. This is your anchor, your personal energy center. (Long pause.)

6. When you've located your anchor, ask yourself how it feels in this place. (Pause.) Do you feel a wave of deep relaxation here? (Pause.) A surge of warmth? (Pause.) A sensation of spaciousness? (Pause.) Any other feeling or sensation? (Longer pause.)

7. Now ask if there's an image that connects you to this part of your body. (Longer pause.)

8. Next, notice if you hear any message for yourself here in your anchor. (Longer pause.)

9. Your anchor is a physical touchstone within your body. Breathe deeply and enjoy this rooted, centered, comfortable spot. (Longer pause.)

10. Now take whatever time you need to recall your divinatory question and then invite your body to receive it, to take it in. (Short

pause.) You could breathe your question in, absorb it through your pores, pick it up with your hands, or let it sink into your body in some other way. (Pause.)

11. Once your body has taken in your query, notice how it feels. (Pause.) Do you detect a shift in energy? A change in comfort level?

12. Where in your body do you feel your oracular question? (Pause.) Travel through your body once again to pinpoint where your divinatory issue has settled. (Long pause.)

13. Now place your attention on this new area of your body, the region where your query dwells. (Pause.) What emotions rise to the surface here? (Pause.) Repeat your divinatory question and let it slowly enter your body again. (Pause.) How does your body respond, especially here in the area where your query resides? (Pause.)

14. Feel into this part of your body where your divinatory question dwells. How does your query manifest here? (Pause.) What sensations do you notice? (Longer pause.) If your question has settled in your neck, for instance, do you feel tension or tugging there? (Pause.) Do you feel any discomfort or confusion in this part of your body? (Pause.) Any yearnings or longings? (Pause.) Do you feel blocked energy, either as pressure, pain, or sluggishness? (Pause.) Any other feelings or sensations? (Pause.) What does your divinatory question feel like? (Pause.) Explore whatever you notice. (Longer pause.)

15. Now return to your anchor, your personal energy center, and invite it to give you a body sense concerning your query. (Pause.) How does your anchor respond to your invitation? (Pause.) What sensations or emotions do you feel? (Longer pause.) Do you feel any tugs or tension here? (Pause.) Any yearnings or longings? (Pause.) Safely held in your personal energy center, how does your query feel now? (Pause.) Explore whatever you notice. (Longer pause.)

16. Now carry the bodily sense you received from your energy center with you into the part of your body where your question resides. Does this new energy from your anchor change your feelings surrounding your issue? How does this part of your body feel now? (Pause.) Has there been some change? (Pause.) Some shift? (Pause.) Does the body sense from your anchor affect the sensations and feelings here in any way? (Longer pause.)

17. Now return to your anchor again, where you feel most rooted, most centered, most comfortable. (Pause.) Spend some time breathing energy from your anchor into the part of your body where your query has settled. (Longer pause.) Do you feel a physical change in the way the question resides in your body now? (Longer pause.)

18. And before you return to your normal reality from this meditation, remember what you experienced. (Short pause.) Recall where to locate your anchor in your body, as well as the image or message that connects you with it. (Short pause.) Remember the body sense you first experienced where your question dwells. (Short pause.) Recall the body sense you intuited in your personal energy center. (Short pause.) And finally, notice how the energy from your anchor affected your original body sense. Notice the differences and how they relate to your issue.

19. And when you're ready, take three deep breaths and slowly come back to your normal reality. Tap your body lightly all over with your fingertips and slowly open your eyes.

20. Record your guided meditation and interpret its meaning. If you don't immediately understand it, use "Common Associations with Physical Locations" (p. 238) and free association (p. 18) to discover its implications.

21. Thank your body for its wisdom.

CONTINUING THE JOURNEY

The first part of this exercise can be especially valuable. Simply remembering your anchor's location plus the image or message that connects you with it will help you return there. This personal energy center can be a resource in many situations. Whenever you're anxious or uncertain, you can withdraw to your anchor, check out whether something feels right or not, and, if necessary, figure out how to regroup.

This body meditation invites you to feel into your oracular issue in several ways: from your anchor; from the place where your query dwells in your body; and, finally, from the combination of the two. One easy way to interpret your divination involves noticing how your body's sensations differed in all of these places. Experiencing your issue from your anchor allows you to let go of your anxieties about your issue, at least for a moment. As science has recently proven, this is a necessary first step in coming to new understandings, since fear locks us into analytical thinking or even "tunnel vision."[A]

In order to help you understand what your body is telling you, I've compiled a list of "Common Associations with Physical Locations" (see Appendix, p. 238). These are just some of the physical responses your feelings or thoughts can arouse. The more acquainted you become with the range of your physical reactions, the simpler it will be for you to use this method of divination. You'll have learned to tap into a more intuitive way of discovering what you're feeling or thinking in situations that might otherwise seem unclear.

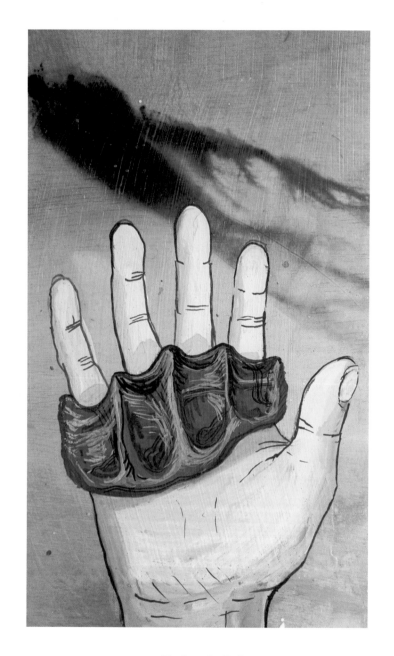

CLAY

SCULPTING YOUR INSIGHT

› BASIC ‹

Most people wouldn't think of sculpting clay as a form of divination, but potters know that their craft transports them to a state that feels more grounded and centered. In fact, Mary Caroline Richards's 1962 book *Centering in Pottery, Poetry, and the Person* has conveyed this idea to many readers.

Grounding and centering can expand or broaden your attention, as I mentioned in chapter 1. In the deeply restful, unfocused state that results, the brain is flooded with alpha waves. Since alpha waves suppress distractions, they allow your mind to retrieve weaker, alternative ideas, freeing you from analytical first impressions. As such, working with clay can help you to think "outside the box."[A]

As I've designed it, **Sculpting Your Insight** offers an oracular technique that will satisfy kinesthetic people, especially those who love to work with their hands. Modeling clay has a wonderful texture and feels cool to the touch when you begin to work it, but warms as it grows more pliable. Best of all, clay is supple enough to take almost any form that your deeper knowing wants to sculpt. And since it comes directly from the earth, it can connect you with the wisdom of our planet—just like your chosen rock in **Hands-On Wisdom**, page 178. If you're drawn to visual oracles, Sculpting Your Insight will appeal to you in two ways: You can feast your eyes on the clay object you've created and study it as an image of the answer you seek.

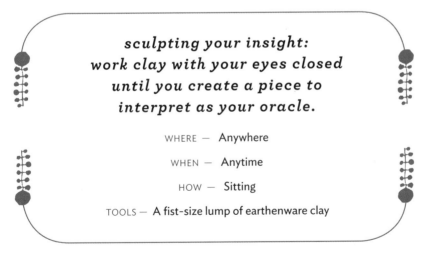

sculpting your insight: work clay with your eyes closed until you create a piece to interpret as your oracle.

WHERE — Anywhere

WHEN — Anytime

HOW — Sitting

TOOLS — A fist-size lump of earthenware clay

With its earthy feel, clay will almost automatically ground you, transporting you to an altered consciousness that facilitates oracular insight. "Opening up" a piece of clay, as potters sometimes call this process, can bring you into the present moment and connect you to your inner depths.

STEPS

1. Buy a lump of earthenware clay about the size of man's fist or double the size of a woman's.

2. Formulate your question (p. 12).

3. Close your eyes and ground and center with the clay in your hands (p. 15). Let the feel of the clay in your hands during your grounding meditation create a space separate from your everyday life and a mind-set free of your ordinary, analytical thinking.

4. Acknowledge the clay you're holding as your oracle.

5. State your question out loud.

6. When you feel the urge, begin to knead the clay, pressing out any bubbles to create a rounded, homogeneous lump ready to mold.

7. When you feel the time is right, remind yourself of your question and, with your eyes still closed, begin to open up the clay in the way it wants to unfold. Follow its lead. Does it need some holes? Or does the clay long to be smoothed? Does it want bits attached to its sides? Or to form a continuous whole?

8. When your piece reaches a natural stopping point, usually in five to ten minutes, open your eyes and add any decorative flourishes that feel appropriate.

9. Study what you've made. Spend some time carefully rolling your sculpted clay in your hands to see all sides of the object. After a few minutes, you will begin to notice that an answer to your question is forming, just as the clay formed in your hands.

10. Interpret your oracle, using free association (p. 18) or the questions in "Continuing the Journey" to unlock its secrets.

11. Thank your sculpture for its insight.

CONTINUING THE JOURNEY

For this divination method, I strongly urge you to use the earthenware clay that children used to play with in school. This type of natural clay comes in red or grayish colors, but in either case, it derives from the earth, and potters use it to make ceramics. Polymer clays like Fimo or Sculpey may make a nicer finished product, but they're stiffer to work with. When you're divining, the process is the point. Earthenware clay works more easily and feels better in your hands. Also, for many of us it's associated with childhood memories, allowing us to access our playful "younger self"[36] while sculpting: This can act as a route to deeper wisdom.

As with any symbolic oracle, you'll need to determine which associations resonate with your experience in order to interpret what you see in your molded clay. While studying it, you can ask yourself these questions:

- What does your molded clay suggest to you?

- What does its shape imply about your question?

- Is it sharp like a knife, indicating a need to cut something?

- Or is it curved and inviting?

- What associations do you have with the image you've created?

- Do these associations relate to any of your recent experiences?

- Do you see smaller symbols contained within the clay?

- How do they relate to each other and to your divinatory question?

- How does the molded clay make you feel?

Once you've finished, you can honor the guidance you've received from your oracle by allowing the clay to dry and then painting or decorating it in whatever way appeals to you. If you place this finished "object of inner wisdom" (see p. 20) where you can see it on a daily basis, it will remind you of the insight you gained from your oracle.

DANCE
ECSTATIC ENLIGHTENMENT

› ADVANCED ‹

Many traditions around the world have recognized dance's powerful spiritual qualities. Native American rituals, like the well-known Sun Dance of the Plains Indians, come immediately to mind. African ceremonies that include dance cover a wide range of purposes, whether it's a Zulu coming-of-age ritual, a Yoruba invocation of the serpent deity Da, or the Ewe dance of life from Ghana. Down under, the *corroboree*, a ceremonial gathering of Aboriginal Australians, involves ritual music and dance as well. Tibetan monks perform *Cham*, the sacred dance of the *vajrayana* Buddhist tradition, while whirling dervishes make up just one of the Sufi orders that dance to enter ecstatic trance. Even early Christian churches participated in liturgical dances, while temple dancers in India still engage in *Bharata Natyam* and other classical dance forms.

Author and activist Jalaja Bonheim, who studied Indian temple dance for many years, suggests that any ecstatic practice needs to alternate movement and quiet, sound and silence, as well as extroversion and introversion. Dancing can awaken you to ecstasy, but to use it for spiritual purposes, you need to turn it inward in order to awaken your intuitive knowledge. Letting the energy raised during the movement sink into the silence of your spiritual core keeps you from dissipating it in the outer world as extraneous gestures or as unnecessary sound. This in turn allows for its use for divination.

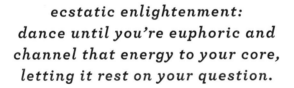

ecstatic enlightenment:
dance until you're euphoric and
channel that energy to your core,
letting it rest on your question.

WHERE — Anywhere

WHEN — Anytime

HOW — Dancing

TOOLS — Comfortable clothes to dance in

A CD of dance music that plays without
a break for ten to fifteen minutes OR

A friend who will drum for you

Like drumming and chanting, dancing is an ancient technique for entering trance (see chapter 1, p. 16). Plus, becoming exhilarated and joyful while moving to music you love will give you a more positive take on your issue and can provide a distraction from the worries associated with it. As recent experiments show, this mood change makes a creative insight more likely. Such a euphoric interlude also functions as a diversion from your query, another practical strategy scientists recommend to allow new ideas to surface.^

When you move to the repetitive rhythms of a drum or to the melody of a powerful chant, your scattered thoughts and feelings begin to coalesce, and you enter a state where body and mind attune to spirit. While dancing, you become one with the essence of the music, a state of mind that can ultimately open and expand so that you merge with your deep knowing.

STEPS

1. Formulate your question (p. 12) and collect your tools.

2. Ground and center (p. 15). Let your meditation create a space separate from your everyday life and a mind-set free of your ordinary, analytical thinking.

3. State your question out loud.

4. Turn on your CD or ask your friend to begin to drum.

5. Dance ecstatically, allowing your body to move continuously in whatever way it desires. Be aware of the rhythmic pulse of the music as it flows through you, becoming gestures and steps. Delight in your body's liveliness and grace. Move sensuously, as if you were making love to life, and let yourself be suffused with the pleasurable sensations you feel.

6. After about five to ten minutes, or maybe less, you'll begin to enter a new awareness, usually an expanded sense of self. Let this trance (see chapter 1, p. 16) deepen as you dance ecstatically for a few more minutes.

7. When you finish dancing, let the energy you've raised sink into your inner depths while either sitting or standing with your eyes closed.

8. Imagine that energy flowing into your question while you remain in a restful, quiet, meditative state. Notice what wisdom emerges for you. Has dancing elicited new insights? Or changed your attitude toward your question? Are you feeling more vigorous and ready to take on your issue? Or simply more relaxed about it? Notice the ways in which your divination has nudged you toward resolution of your quandary.

9. Take note of your divinatory outcome.

10. Interpret your oracle, possibly using free association (p. 18).

11. Thank the dancing for your oracle.

CONTINUING THE JOURNEY

Before you begin a dance oracle, always make sure that you're wearing comfortable clothing, and then dance until you feel vibrant and alive, even ecstatic. This kind of divination depends on reaching at least the threshold of this blissful state. You can arrive at this consciousness most easily if you use music that uplifts you. It also helps if the music plays continuously for the entire ten to fifteen minutes, so that you can dance without a break.

Most people find it difficult to remember their query while dancing. That's okay: Simply remind yourself of your question when you've finished dancing. Then, in the moments or minutes of silence and anticipatory glow that follow, your answer will arrive.

In order to experience ecstasy, you have to relinquish control, so your first experience of such euphoria may be disorienting. If this is the case for you, don't be discouraged. Simply dance again when you feel ready. I think you'll be glad you gave it a second try, for as Jalaja Bonheim writes, "In every moment, the real and the possible dance together within the ground of our being, and out of this dance the future is born."

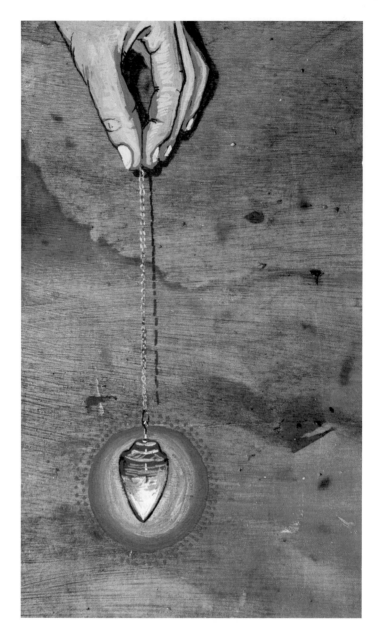

DOWSING

DIVINING WITH FINGERS AND THUMBS

› BASIC ‹

Most people know dowsing as a technique for sensing underground water. But, more broadly, this term refers to amplifying the knowledge of the body in order to obtain the answer to an either/or question. Dowsing depends on the ideomotor effect—the slight involuntary movements each of us makes in response to various stimuli. When we dowse, we rely on the wisdom of our bodies as indicated through these movements.

As a divinatory technique, dowsing has existed for millennia. In fact, the Tassili-n-Ajjer caves in Saharan Algeria hold an 8,000-year-old pictograph depicting a shaman with a Y-shaped rod in his hands, searching for water in this extremely dry region. As early as the third millennium BCE, history lists Emperor Yu, the founder of the Hsi Dynasty in China, as the first recorded dowser. Dowsing figured prominently in Chinese politics again 5,000 years later. When forced to flee Tibet by the invading Chinese, the Dalai Lama, the spiritual leader of Tibetan Buddhism, had to decide whether to travel the short distance to Bhutan or climb through the Himalayan Mountains for over forty miles to India. He used a form of dowsing to make his choice: He closed his eyes, raised his arms in front of him to chest level, and then attempted to touch the tips of his forefingers together. When they met, his divination indicated he should escape to India.[c]

divining with fingers and thumbs:
press the thumb and pinkie
of your nondominant hand
together and try to break the contact
with your dominant index finger to
answer an either/or question.

WHERE — **Anywhere**

WHEN — **Anytime**

HOW — **Sitting or standing**

TOOLS — **Your hands**

Divining with Fingers and Thumbs offers a versatile form of dowsing since it uses nothing but your hands. When in doubt, you can quickly assess any situation just by trying to pull your fingers apart. But it's important to remember that dowsing, even more than most oracles, requires you to let go of any preconceived notions about the best outcome: It's easy to affect the results of such an oracle through slight differences in how you hold your hands, pull your fingers, and so on. In fact, Sig Lonegren, one of the leading practitioners of dowsing, recommends that diviners using this type of divination assume the manner of a child discovering beautifully wrapped presents.[c] If you approach your dowsing oracles with this childlike sense of wonder, then you're bound to have successful experiences with this technique.

STEPS

1. Formulate an either/or question (p. 12).

2. Ground and center (p. 15). Let your meditation create a space separate from your everyday life and a mind-set free of your ordinary, analytical thinking.

3. Press the thumb and pinkie of your nondominant hand together in a circle.

4. Ask your question out loud.

5. Curl the index finger of your dominant hand and thread it through the circle you've created. Pull directly on the point of the circle where the pinkie and thumb connect, but don't twist your nondominant hand or make any deliberate attempt to break the contact between your thumb and pinkie.

6. If you separate your thumb and pinkie, your answer is no. If you don't break the circle, your answer is yes.

7. Thank your hands for your oracle.

CONTINUING THE JOURNEY

Dowsing may seem like a minor form of divination since it can only answer yes-or-no questions. But in the same way that computers repeatedly use the numbers zero and one to perform fairly complicated functions, you too can ask a series of either/or questions to establish the answer to a more complex inquiry. After all, we live in the digital age, so why not digitize! It's simply a matter of coming up with the right questions. But you need to be careful with your follow-up questions. Don't restate your query, making sure in this way that you're not trying to manipulate the outcome of your oracle.

The simplicity of this technique is one of its greatest strengths. I'm a non-kinesthetic diviner and can attest that this technique works for those of us who aren't adept at kinesthetic oracles, since it's uncomplicated and straightforward. I discovered dowsing's versatility when I returned from England and Ireland in 1997. During my travels, I had discovered the power of ley lines and, as a result, I wanted to plot their location in my Madison, Wisconsin, neighborhood. These earth energy paths correspond to the meridians of Chinese medicine, but instead of running through the body, they plot the course of energy on the earth's surface. Where two or more cross, there's an energy vortex similar to a chakra in the human body.

I lived near some sites I considered sacred and wanted to discover if they were located on ley lines like the stone circles and holy wells that I visited in England and Ireland. I had seen dowsing rods in England but had no idea where to buy them in the United States, so I called my friend Jade, author of the book *To Know*, an early book on Wiccan magic. She told me that I already knew how to dowse. Still, I was clueless. Then she replied that all I needed to do was use my pendulum—a small, heavy object hanging from a chain or string that amplifies your body knowledge—asking, "Am I standing on a ley line?" The pendulum would answer "Yes" or "No."

Surprisingly, when I located the ley lines in my neighborhood, the answer to my question—whether the springs I considered holy stood on an intersection of ley lines—turned out to be "Close, but no cigar." Two ley lines converged on each other (less than a yard apart), but they didn't cross.

EARTH

HANDS-ON WISDOM

› ADVANCED ‹

For the ancient Greeks, from whom we inherit our understanding of the elements, earth represented the physical. As an element, it has a lot to do with our bodies and the possibility of inhabiting them in a truly grounded manner. Viewed in this way, earth lends itself to a kinesthetic approach to divination.

Earth links us with family and friends since we are most physically "in touch" with them. It also connects us with nature in a visceral way and with the many life forms that have existed on our planet. For me, rocks and soil provide the best symbols of this element: rocks, because they comprise the oldest artifacts created by Mother Earth, and soil, because it sustains life for all the creatures who live here, including human beings.

Perhaps more than any other nations, the diverse communities of American Indians have revered the "stone people," a name given to rocks and boulders by Native Americans. Tsalagi (Cherokee) elders in both the eastern and western parts of North America use crystals and stones in their divinations. Among the Numakiki (Mandan) Indians in North Dakota, medicine rocks foretell the happenings of the coming year when consulted in the spring. And in the north-central United States, the Lakota set aside time to search for rocks that "speak" to them. Naturally occurring designs on these spirit rocks are used to guide them in their lives.[c]

While cradling your chosen rock during **Hands-On Wisdom**, you, too, will begin to feel grounded. In most cases, this will allow you to let go of your anxieties

hands-on wisdom: as you feel the weight and texture of a large rock in your hands, let your mind drift to your question and see what surfaces.

WHERE — **Anywhere**

WHEN — **Anytime**

HOW — **Sitting**

TOOLS — **A fist-size or larger rock**

concerning your issue. Neuroscientists have recently begun to suggest that anxiety blocks creative insights and keeps you inside your "mental box" when you want to think outside of it. Lessening worry while holding your rock can induce a "brain blink," which in turn can lead to an aha moment.[A]

I created this oracular method as a means of literally getting in touch with your issue. You may choose a rock that's dear to you or one that you've just seen for the first time. As you walk through a natural area, a stone may also "choose you," so to speak, by catching your eye due to its shape, color, or some other quality. Practice scanning the ground as you walk, and one will call out to you.

Since Earth's geology has witnessed events over millions, even billions, of years, Her stones have a lot to teach us. One of the lessons we can learn using this oracular method is to take our problems less seriously, since the life span of a human being constitutes but a blink of an eye in comparison with geologic time.

STEPS

1. Locate your divinatory rock.

2. Formulate your question (p. 12).

3. Ground and center (p. 15). Let your meditation create a space separate from your everyday life and a mind-set free of your ordinary, analytical thinking.

4. Cradle the rock you've selected in your hands and acknowledge it as your oracle.

5. If you haven't done so already, close your eyes and then silently state your question.

6. Now feel the weight and texture of the rock for five to ten minutes. As you sense its bulges and cavities, its smooth areas and rough edges, the fineness or coarseness of its exterior, find the position that best fits your hands. Then let your mind drift from your question to your rock's solidity and heaviness. Attune

yourself to its physicality. Sense how your body responds by sinking into a deeper state of relaxation as you meditate with your rock.

7. After meditating for five to ten minutes, repeat your question silently to yourself.

8. Meditate a few minutes more if you have yet to receive an oracle.

9. Interpret your divination, perhaps with the help of free association (p. 18).

10. Thank your rock for your oracle.

CONTINUING THE JOURNEY

You can begin this divination by walking in a scenic area—in the woods or by a lakeshore, perhaps—until a stone catches your eye. Sitting in the stone's natural environment may open you to the wisdom of this kinesthetic technique more easily than performing it at home.

But **Hands-On Wisdom** can work in either setting. For instance, I recently walked through my house until a rock attracted my attention, and then sat at my desk while holding it. After becoming attuned to the rock's qualities, its weight, and the feel of its surface, I rolled it around until I found the position that best fit my hands. Hands-On Wisdom not only calmed me down enough to ground and center—an almost automatic response to such a weighty object—but it also allowed me to realize a very physical answer to my question. The comfort of the rock in my left hand began to resonate with the rhythm of my breathing, and I realized what I needed. I had been wondering how to forgive myself after my elderly mother's ill-fated visit. While she was in my house, I'd tried to provide her with some stimulation and activities of interest to her when—as I realized later— all she really wanted was a steady routine with no changes in her schedule. What seeped into my consciousness as I held my rock was that I needed to breathe deeply and peacefully. With that awareness, I realized that I could let go of any residual feelings of guilt by gradually releasing them—one exhalation at a time.

HANDS AND FEET
YOUR BODY'S SIGNALS

› ADVANCED ‹

Paleontologists have recently theorized that *Homo sapiens* matured as a species because we walked upright on our feet, freeing our hands for other tasks. In fact, scientists believe that the human hand and brain coevolved and that the development of opposable thumbs led to our ability to create tools, language, and other aspects of complex intelligence.[37]

So it's no wonder that hands and feet have been honored by the world's religions. Within Taoism, these appendages contain important energy centers—"bubbling wells" in the feet and "working temples" in the hands—that play a principal role in the movement of vital energy or qi within the body.[38] The Hindu energy system also concludes that hands and feet contain the most important secondary chakras after the seven major centers. For this reason, Hindu devotees touch their guru's feet, just as Christ's disciples washed His.[39]

*your body's signals:
notice where your feet want
to take you or what your hands
want to do as a pathway to
greater insight into your issue.*

WHERE — **Anywhere**

WHEN — **Anytime**

HOW — **Walking**

TOOLS — **A place to observe your body's signals**

Tara, the Hindu Goddess and Tibetan *bodhisattva* (enlightened being), has seven eyes: the two that you and I possess, plus a "third eye" in the middle of her forehead; one on each palm; and one on the sole of each foot. The last four "eyes" in Her hands and feet intrigued me. Reflecting on Tara one day, I wondered if my hands and feet ever conveyed the depth of understanding that Hers seemed to symbolize. After considering this for a while, I realized that the answer was yes.

I often walked directly toward an object I needed at a particular moment without first thinking about where I was going, or I'd reach out a hand, without any conscious thought, to retrieve something I had lost. I believe we all have this latent potential, especially those of us who are kinesthetically connected to our world. Using it can give us insight into our dilemmas.

STEPS

1. Decide on the location in which you want to notice **Your Body's Signals**.

2. Formulate your question (p. 12).

3. Ground and center (p. 15). Let your meditation create a space separate from your everyday life and a mind-set free of your ordinary, analytical thinking.

4. Standing with your eyes closed, remind yourself of your question.

5. When it feels right, open your eyes and notice where your feet want to take you or what your hands want to do. Does your head incline in a certain direction, indicating where you want to go? Do you feel an impulse to move in a certain way, implying a method for dealing with your issue? Is there an action you want to perform? Observe both the path you take and its goal.

6. Notice also what your hands want to do. Do they reach out for an object or a person, indicating the need for some help with your query? Do they shield you in some way, perhaps from an undesirable outcome? Are there things your hands want to touch or objects they want to avoid? What are they? Are your hands making any gestures? What kind?

7. Interpret your oracle, possibly using free association (p. 18).

8. Thank your body for its wisdom.

CONTINUING THE JOURNEY

It's best to undertake this technique outside, but you can also use it within four walls. And, depending on your divination, you'll need to analyze your experience by examining the symbol(s) that appear. Sometimes the path you trace will clarify your situation. In other cases, a symbolic object, a gesture, a person, a feeling, an intention, or an activity will offer a response to your predicament. If you can identify the association(s) you have with these symbols, what your oracle has to tell you will soon become clear. Sometimes your inner insight will act out its wisdom in an obvious manner, and sometimes its meaning may seem almost imperceptible—just a subtle shift in the way you perceive your situation.

In a variation on this technique, you can combine **Your Body's Signals** with a chant to Tara, who inspired this divination method. Tara represents the Great Mother of Tibetan Buddhism, who vowed to be reincarnated as a woman until all people reach enlightenment. Especially if you're auditory, singing Her name requests Her aid while also allowing you to become more present to Her guidance and your own insight. If you wish to move both your vocal cords and your feet, simply chant to Tara as you walk. Singing the traditional Tibetan chant "Om Tara Tu Tara" often proves the best choice. You can find it on my recording *Chants for the Queen of Heaven* as well as in several songbooks. (See "Chanting and Other Music" in Resources, p. 226.)

Here's a personal example to help you understand how this divination works. While rewriting this entry, I realized that I felt a little blue. So I asked my inner wisdom what would best lift me out of my Wisconsin winter blahs. As soon as I formulated my question—and before I had even opened my eyes—my legs turned me around in my office chair to face the door of my study. The movement of my body felt exhilarating (and perhaps that was part of the answer to my question). With my eyes open, I walked out into the hallway and turned toward my meditation room. But my feet didn't step up into it. Instead, they continued to amble around the hallway until I stood opposite the stairway. As soon as I looked downstairs, my feet hurried down the steps and took me directly to the front door, where my hand swung out to grasp the doorknob. Soon afterward, I went outside for a walk. I felt immediate relief as I took my first steps and breathed in the fresh, crisp air. After I had walked a couple blocks, I also realized that meditating might also help to return me to a sunny mood.

JOURNALING
THIRD-PAGE DIVINATION

› BASIC ‹

Many early cultures viewed knowledge and the written words that recorded it as divine. Such thinking may be as ancient as the Hindu Goddess Saraswati. Saraswati, whom Indians still venerate today, came to India with the Vedic priests around 3000 BCE and ever since has been the Goddess of music, prayer, and writing. For Her devotees, writing represents a manifestation of the Divine.

Ancient Mesopotamians,[40] Mayans, and Egyptians also had myths that portrayed writing as holy. In Egypt, the Goddess Seshat linked writing and divination, as well as wisdom. As Mistress of the House of Books, She was most often pictured as a scribe and record keeper.[41]

In the West, the use of writing for divinatory purposes began with the Spiritualists. Starting in the nineteenth century, they used "spirit writing" to contact deceased loved ones, lending comfort to those left behind. (Spirit writing was also found in China—and continues in Taiwan today—where Gods are believed to take over a stylus and write instructions for their worshipers.[D]) During the 1920s, Surrealist writers and artists in Paris invented "automatic writing" as a means of contacting the unconscious as a source of artistic inspiration. They would write as rapidly as possible in order to move from conscious to unconscious control,[42] just as you should while performing a **Third-Page Divination**.

third-page divination: using an adapted version of julia cameron's "morning pages," tap into your creative flow and find new ways of approaching your issue.

WHERE — Anywhere

WHEN — Anytime

HOW — Sitting

TOOLS — 3 sheets of 8½" x 11" (21.5 × 28 cm) paper (or a journal with the same dimensions)

A pen or pencil

The purpose of the Third-Page Divination is "flow writing," a method for discovering your wisdom underneath the "mental box" of surface thinking. As author and speaker Christina Baldwin writes, "Flow writing is the tip of the iceberg, touching on thoughts that ride deeply in your mind."[1]

My favorite journaling technique is the practice of "morning pages" suggested in Julia Cameron's book *The Artist's Way*, a method that I modified for myself as a daily oracle. Cameron directs readers to fill three 8½" x 11" (21.5 × 28 cm) sheets every morning before their day begins as a means of aiding their creative flow. Since "flow"[43] is exactly the state you want to achieve in order to enter into the mystery of an oracle, here I've combined the "stream-of-consciousness" writing Cameron recommends in the first two of those pages with a final page in which you ask your inner wisdom to answer your oracular question.

STEPS

1. Collect your tools.

2. Formulate your question (p. 12).

3. Ground and center (p. 15). Let your meditation create a space separate from your everyday life and a mind-set free of your ordinary, analytical thinking.

4. When it feels right, begin to write whatever comes into your head. Write rapidly and allow the words to flow. The first two pages don't have to have anything to do with your oracular query.

5. After completing the second sheet of paper, write your question at the top of the third sheet. You may wish to address your question to a particular person, deity, or spirit guide.

6. Write a response to your question on this final sheet, allowing your inner knowing to answer your query. If at first you don't know what to write, just keep your hand moving: Write whatever comes into your mind until something percolates up from your unconscious. Don't stop the movement of writing from the beginning to the end of this oracle.

7. Reread the final sheet for the wisdom you seek. If you still haven't answered your question, write on the back of the third page (or on the top of a new page in your journal): "I trust my inner wisdom to answer me regarding _____," filling in the blank with a shortened form of your query. Then write for another page. If you feel stuck, rewrite over and over again, "I trust my inner wisdom to answer me regarding _____" until you notice an answer to your query forming.

8. Interpret your oracle, perhaps with free association (p. 18).

9. Thank your inner scribe for your oracle.

CONTINUING THE JOURNEY

While performing a **Third-Page Divination**, every now and then you'll discover that your inner scribe answers the question that underlies your issue rather than your query itself. Sometimes you will find that this wisdom is more useful than a straightforward answer. If not, you may want to journal again the following day.

Keeping an oracular journal can be empowering. The more you undertake **Journaling** oracles, the more you learn to trust your inner guidance. You also learn more and more about your spiritual journey through life. As psychologist Ralph Metzner wrote, "The completed [spiritual] journey always ends with a return, a home-coming to the ordinary world of conventional reality that was left behind. This world has been transformed, if our journey [or journaling, I might add] has been successful, into a new world, seen with fresh eyes. The end of the journey is the beginning of a new, empowered way of life."[44] You can remind yourself of this by leaving your oracular journal open to the page of your current divination so you can read it from time to time.

This form of "morning pages" has become a daily divination method for me. Even after many years, I'm amazed by how much insight I gain from what I pen on that third sheet of paper each day. Since my daily question is "How shall I live today?" my inner guide will sometimes give me practical suggestions for how to structure my day. But more often than not—and more importantly—She tells me how to find joy on that particular day.

MEDITATION
MINDFUL KNOWING

› ADVANCED ‹

Since the late 1960s when the Maharishi Mahesh Yogi introduced the Beatles to transcendental meditation, the popularity of meditative practices has grown in the West. Meditation has become part of mainstream religion and medicine, and its mental and physical benefits have been proven by scientific studies. It's especially effective in reducing stress.[45]

Although we associate meditation with Eastern spiritual traditions, in the West, Judaism, Christianity, and Islam have each encouraged contemplative techniques for gaining direct experience of the divine as well: meditation and prayer within Christianity; kabbalistic and Hasidic practices within Judaism; and *dhikr* in Islam—a devotional technique involving repetition of phrases from the Qur'an, Islamic aphorisms, or the ninety-nine "Names of God."

In contrast to the West, the East has emphasized meditative practices for millennia. Those best known in the West include mindfulness, mantra meditation, *qigong*, the use of koans—which are seemingly nonsensical problems meant to challenge the mind to see reality as it truly is—and, more recently, Tantric meditation.[F]

Meditative techniques can be invaluable when you're searching for inner clarity about an oracular question. As author and meditation teacher James Baraz says, "Practicing mindfulness disrupts our habitual patterns of thinking. Instead of reacting on automatic pilot, we have a choice." These are almost the

mindful knowing: calmly follow your breath as it deepens and slows, allowing your mind to find greater clarity about your issue.

WHERE — A quiet place

WHEN — Anytime

HOW — Sitting

TOOLS — A quiet place to meditate

same words used by neuroscientists to describe how sudden insights help us to see things in a new light.[A] This ability of meditation to facilitate "outside-the-box thinking" is the reason I adapted mindfulness as a divination technique.

As a form of grounding and centering, meditation can also help you when you perform any type of oracle, and it has long-term benefits as well. Meditating daily, twice daily, or even weekly will help open your mind to your own wise guidance while decreasing the tension in your life. I highly recommend it as a regular practice.

Mindfulness is probably the most straightforward meditation technique. At its simplest, it involves following your breath with the ultimate purpose of investigating the mind-body experience on a moment-to-moment basis. When your mind starts to wander—as it invariably will—use it as an opportunity to gently bring your attention back to your breath. Unless, of course, you've received oracular guidance that you want to immediately capture. Then it's best to end your divination, remind yourself of what you've learned, and thank your inner wisdom for its counsel.

STEPS

1. Find a quiet place where you won't be interrupted.

2. Formulate your question (p. 12).

3. Sit comfortably. If you're sitting in a chair, make sure to plant your feet firmly on the ground about shoulder-width apart. Also, soften your neck and lengthen your spine in a relaxed way so that your head rests gently on top of your vertebrae. This will also allow your shoulders to drop and your breath to deepen.

4. State your question out loud.

5. Follow your breathing by thinking to yourself, "I am breathing in," as you inhale, and "I am breathing out," as you exhale.

6. Gently observe how your breathing deepens and slows, relaxing you into a more peaceful place.

7. After a few minutes, notice how awareness of your breath allows you to be in the present moment instead of rehashing the issues surrounding your question or worrying about the future. Here, time becomes spacious and life opens out into the infinite.

8. When your mind wanders back to your issue or to other thoughts, delicately nudge it back to your breathing.

9. After tuning out the distractions of your mind by meditating for ten to fifteen minutes, return to your oracular question in order to experience it with a fresh mind-set. Within a few minutes, you will sense an answer to your query.

10. Interpret the outcome. If it has arrived as a symbol or feeling, you may need to use free association (p. 18) to analyze its meaning.

11. If you need further clarification, meditate again sometime in the next few days.

12. Thank your inner guidance for your oracle.

CONTINUING THE JOURNEY

While meditating, you might prefer to count your breaths instead of thinking, "I am breathing in," and "I am breathing out." In either case, your goal is to allow your attention to alight on your breath as a doorway to the vibrancy of your life and, by the same token, to the many possibilities it offers.

Gently discovering the reverberant silence within the noise in your life is the aim of mindfulness. As you meditate, you let your mind attend to something other than your question and, as a result, allow your unconscious to incubate an answer to your oracular issue—another scientifically proven technique for eliciting an insight.[A] For this reason, once you have finished meditating, new approaches to your question often appear.

MUDRAS

TOUCHING SPIRIT WITH FINGER YOGA

› ADVANCED ‹

Mudras are special hand positions used in Hinduism and Buddhism to invoke a variety of energies and qualities. If you examine artwork representing Eastern deities, you'll notice these finger gestures on many of the statues and paintings. These symbolic poses resemble *asanas*, the postures employed in yoga—but instead of the entire body, they involve only the hands. As a result, you might call them finger yoga.

Mudras represent diverse states of consciousness. Hindu and Buddhist devotees generally use mudras during meditation to influence different parts of the brain or the body. Just as reflexology maps the foot, the practice of mudras assumes that each part of the hands mirrors an area of the body or mind. Mudras' capacities have their roots in the physiology of the fingertips, which have an extensive network of nerve endings as well as multiple energy channels. For this reason, mudras can transfer information to the brain and other energy centers.[46]

The major sources of information about mudras come from the classical texts of Hatha Yoga, the *Hatha Yoga Pradipika* and the *Gherand Samhita*. Written between the fifteenth and seventeenth centuries, these yogic manuals also describe the asanas, breathing techniques, the chakras, and much more.

Mudras can help people come to terms with their past, recharge their energy reserves, improve relationships, solve everyday problems, and support the healing of chronic conditions.[J] Each finger is associated with one of the five elements in yoga (earth, air, fire, water, and space), allowing mudra positions to affect and

touching spirit with finger yoga:
assume the jnana mudra
to facilitate your understanding
of a situation in your life.

WHERE — **Anywhere**

WHEN — **Anytime**

HOW — **Lying down or sitting**

TOOLS — **Hands**

balance these building blocks of the body and mind. Hatha yoga employs twenty-four mudras, while Kundalini yoga has one hundred and eight.

The technique described here draws on the *jnana* mudra, a general-purpose mudra also called *chin* or *guyan* that you can use for any oracular question.[J] In this mudra, the thumb symbolizes the cosmic or divine wisdom while the index finger designates the individual or human spirit. At the same time, the thumb signifies intuition and the index finger indicates inspiration. Since it represents the desire for unifying human and cosmic consciousness, as well as combining intuition and inspiration, using the jnana mudra can help you attain your deepest knowing.

Using a mudra to perform a divination is my own modification of this ancient Eastern practice. As far as I know, traditional Hindus and Buddhists don't normally employ mudras for oracular purposes. But I've found that undertaking a breathing meditation while holding a particular mudra can facilitate your understanding of situations in your life or answer a specific divinatory question. Like all meditative oracles gathered here, **Mudras** depends on a "brain blink" in the occipital lobe of the brain.[^] This sudden disconnect from the outer world diverts awareness from your surroundings, reducing distractions so your mind can become aware of less obvious thoughts.

If you wait while positively anticipating that you will receive the intuition and inspiration you have invoked, you will often receive an answer within a very short period of time, if not during the meditation itself. This type of oracle is especially appropriate for people who not only have kinesthetic tendencies, but also enjoy more advanced oracles.

STEPS

1. Formulate your question (p. 12).

2. Ground and center (p. 15). Let your meditation create a space separate from your everyday life and a mind-set free of your ordinary, analytical thinking.

3. Sit or lie comfortably, and then inhale and exhale deeply and slowly two or three times. After these purifying breaths, allow your breathing to become deeper and slower.

4. State your question silently to yourself.

5. Assume the jnana mudra as illustrated on page 194. Hold the thumb and index finger of each hand lightly together in a circle, while extending the three other fingers in a relaxed way. Rest your palms facing upward on your thighs. If you have difficulty using both hands while performing this mudra, you may use one hand to hold the fingers of the other in the proper position.

6. Notice the gentle pressure between your thumb and forefinger in this mudra position.

7. Breathe calmly and meditatively.

8. While breathing out, press your thumb and forefinger gently together. While breathing in, let go of this slight pressure. (Focusing on the mudra, specifically on the points between the thumb and forefinger, takes the place of focusing on the breath, as in the **Mindful Knowing** technique on p. 192.)

9. Meditate with warm anticipation of receiving an answer to your question. Smile, knowing that your fingers are inviting intuition and inspiration to arrive.

10. Once you have meditated for about ten to fifteen minutes, relax your hands in your lap and await your oracle.

11. If necessary, ask your question under your breath once again, trusting that you will receive an answer.

12. Thank your hands for your oracle.

13. Interpret your divination, possibly using free association (p. 18).

CONTINUING THE JOURNEY

Sometimes you may need patience and persistence to access your inner wisdom. When this is the case, it's a good idea to meditate the next day using your mudra once more. By then your mind will usually have settled into greater resonance with your deeper self, and guidance may flow almost before you begin. Be gentle with yourself, and your innermost thoughts will express themselves in their own time and their own way.

It's possible to use the **Finger Yoga** technique with mudras other than the jnana gesture, customizing your divination by using mudras that invoke specific states of consciousness. My favorite book on the subject is Gertrud Hirschi's *Mudras: Yoga in Your Hands.*[J] It outlines hundreds of mudras for a wide variety of purposes.

Alternatively, you may want to use your intuition to find a hand gesture that feels appropriate for your question.[F] I used Hirschi's book recently to find a mudra that would help answer the question of whether to reincorporate music into my life while working on this book. Writing was taking a lot of my time, so I had put my musical activities on the back burner. But I missed composing and performing. I had also begun to realize that, although writing stimulates my creative expression, music seemed to prime my creative pump in a deeper way. I decided to use the *ushas* mudra for this question, since it represents creativity and enthusiasm.

After intertwining my fingers with the left thumb on top of the right— assuming the *ushas* mudra (though if you're a man, you should clasp your hands together in such a way that the right thumb lies above the left)—and meditating for ten to twelve minutes, an answer came. I heard "Music will add joy to your life" in my mind. So I called the music director at First Unitarian Society, where I'm a member, and asked him to schedule me to sing in the future. I'm happy that I did: Singing at First Unitarian gladdened my spirit, which promoted my creativity even more than the music itself.

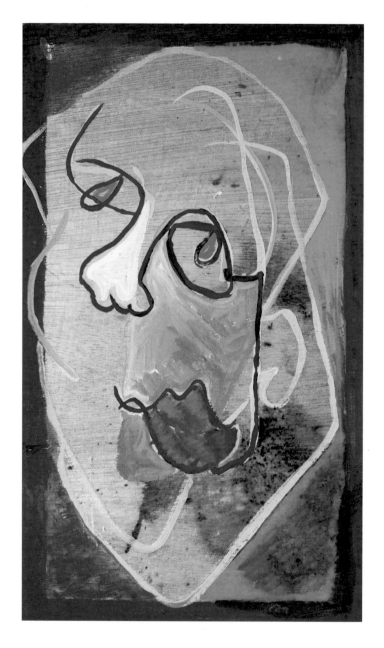

PAINTING AND DRAWING
CREATIVITY UNLEASHED

› BASIC ‹

During the 1920s and 1930s, Surrealist artists used a number of so-called automatic techniques to free their imagination, among them automatic drawing. With these improvisational practices, they hoped to connect with the unconscious as a source of inspiration. They believed that using such unplanned procedures would allow the psyche to reveal material that might otherwise remain repressed. Recently, scientists have proven that this type of unfocused attention *does* facilitate creative connections with the unconscious.[A]

In describing automatic drawing, André Masson, who pioneered the process, noted that the hand should move randomly across the paper, freeing the resulting picture from conscious control. Interestingly, Masson admitted that his automatic drawings involved a two-step process very similar to the divination technique outlined here. First he drew unconsciously, and when his images began to suggest certain kinds of forms, he would outline and embellish them.[47]

creativity unleashed:
let your hand move across the paper
in whatever way feels best
and then interpret what you've
drawn as your oracle.

WHERE — **Anywhere**

WHEN — **Anytime**

HOW — **Sitting**

TOOLS — **Paper**

Pencil, crayons, markers, or paints and brushes

Artist Samantha Snyder, who created a website devoted to doodling, writes that when she draws, she feels all her stress drain out through the tip of her pen. If you've read the first chapter of this book, you'll know she's describing one of the preliminary steps for a good divination.

STEPS

1. Collect your tools.

2. Formulate your question (p. 12).

3. Ground and center (p. 15). Let your meditation create a space separate from your everyday life and a mind-set free of your ordinary, analytical thinking.

4. When the time feels right, pick up your pencil (pen, marker, crayon, chalk, brush, or your paint-covered fingertip) and begin to move it across the paper in whatever way feels best.

5. Draw as if you were doodling. Let your hand go where it wants to go for as long as you feel like it.

6. Add whatever artistic flourishes, embellishments, or ornaments feel appropriate. For instance, you could outline or emphasize parts of your design or change the color of your ink or crayon.

7. At some point, an image or images will begin to emerge. Highlight it (or them) so that you can recognize it later. Add color if you want.

8. Interpret your doodle. First, examine the lines you've drawn. Are some of them light, indicating feelings of tentativeness about your issue? Or are they heavy, implying some strength and resolve? Did any lines tear through the page, pointing toward anger or frustration? Do you see any sharp zigzags, perhaps illustrating some harshness or worry? Or are the lines wavy, giving you the idea that things are fluid or watery? The lines might tell you something about your underlying feelings in the situation.

9. Now notice the position of the object(s) in your drawing. Placement might tell you something about their relative significance. Because of the left-to-right orientation of writing in our culture, something on the left side of the sheet might indicate the past, while the right might imply the future.

10. If you've used colors, they might also help you make sense of your doodle. Finally, freely associate (p. 18) concerning each item and its relationships to the other symbols.[48]

11. Thank the drawing for your oracle.

CONTINUING THE JOURNEY

Interpreting your doodle is like analyzing any other visual image. Don't rush to judgment, but let your eye take in every part of your drawing or painting. When you're done, you'll have an "object of inner wisdom" (see p. 20). Place it in your house or office where it will remind you often of your insight.

Here's something to remember while performing a **Creativity Unleashed** divination: If a phrase or song comes into your mind during the process, it becomes part of the oracle. This happened recently to me. My question was, "How can I facilitate my work while remaining healthy and happy?" I began doodling what turned out to be a female figure with three or four saw-toothed lines next to her head. Soon my pen was swooping in circular motions all over the page, ending in little eddies at the bottom of the sheet. During this part of the drawing, I began to hear the old Cris Williamson song "Filling up and spilling over, it's an endless waterfall." As soon as I tuned into the song, I knew what I had been sketching: I was filling up and spilling over with the love and energy of the universe. I realized that the female figure represented me and that next to my head was a lot of jagged worry noise. The doodle indicated that if I remained open to the love and energy of the universe, I would be able to work creatively, remain healthy, and stay happy, because this energy would flow through me into all areas of my life. If I was able to "go with the flow," then I could let go of my nagging worries.

You don't have to be an artist to use this divination technique. Take it from me: Even as a child, I never considered myself to be very "good at" art. As a result, it surprised me when I looked through my old graduate school notebooks and noticed the doodles in the margins. If I'd known then that my scribblings contained insightful messages, I would have realized much sooner that I was questioning whether academia was the right place for me. Many of my drawings had arrows pointing in different directions. I was asking myself, "Should I go in this direction? Or that way? Or maybe somewhere else?"

SACRED SITES
CONNECTING TO SOURCE

› ADVANCED ‹

Since prehistoric times, people have consecrated sacred sites on mountains, in caves, near rivers and springs, and within temples and churches. Divinations were performed at such sites all over the world. Ancient Greek temples hosted dream divinations, tree omens, and the famous Delphic oracle itself.[49] In Africa, Asia, and pre-Columbian America, approaching an ancestor for guidance often occurred on hallowed ground and, in many of these regions, still does today. In numerous religions, devotees make pilgrimages to these sacred sites, where prayer or other forms of worship occur.

As I've created it, a **Sacred Site** divination is open-ended and dependent on the ability to let go of the fixed ideas you have about your query. This is what neuroscientists call "fixation forgetting." Visiting a sacred site enlarges your perspective from your small, personal point of view—in which you've become stuck—to include a much larger, sacred frame of reference. Broadening your outlook in this way allows you to release your anxiety about your issue. Then your unconscious can look at the bigger picture—in this case, the sacred picture—and discover new ideas.[A]

connecting to source:
open yourself to the wisdom of the
sacred site you have chosen.

WHERE — A sacred site

WHEN — Anytime

HOW — Sitting, standing, or lying down

TOOLS — A place sacred to you

In my experience, three types of holy sites exist. The first type includes places that are sacred to individuals and makes up the most common category. These locations become hallowed because something important happened to the person there—either formative experiences or special events. These might include locations in your childhood neighborhood, the place you met your partner, the site of an outstanding achievement, or spots near your home that have some sort of personal significance to you.

Repeated ceremonies characterize the second type of sacred sites. These include temples, churches, synagogues, sacred groves, holy wells, and other outdoor spaces where people have undertaken rituals or services for many years.

Finally, a third type of sacred site is characterized by the presence of ley lines, or what Chinese *feng shui* masters call "dragon lines." Such energy channels form the earth's counterpart to meridians, the energy pathways in the human body according to Chinese medicine. Where these ley lines cross, they create powerful currents on the earth's surface, like the chakras in the human body. All of these places defined by ley lines connect us with the holiness of the earth and center us in our relationship with the divine. I first experienced several of them in 1997 when I visited stone circles like Stonehenge and Avebury.

In order to perform this divination, first you need to decide which type of sacred site you want to visit. If your query has to do with formative experiences or other personal incidents, seek out a place that's sacred to you as an individual, such as a childhood haunt or another location with important private memories. If your question doesn't relate to any of your personal places of power, you need to think about whether it's better to visit a place where ley lines cross, or one that has been made sacred by human activity. And finally, you'll need to decide whether you prefer a quiet indoor site or a natural setting.

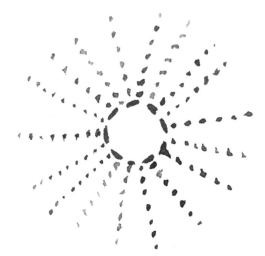

STEPS

1. Formulate your question (p. 12).

2. Go to the sacred site you have chosen.

3. Ground and center while sitting, standing, or lying at your chosen site (p. 15). Let your meditation create a space separate from your everyday life and a mind-set free of your ordinary, analytical thinking.

4. Ask your question out loud.

5. Continue to sit, stand, or lie down in a relaxed and meditative fashion while opening yourself to the wisdom of this place. Feel into this sacred site as you meditate. Breathe your question into your surroundings and let them affect you. Let the sights, sounds, and ambience of this place transport you to greater receptivity. If you're outside, let the breeze and the birdsong open you to new ideas. If you're inside, let the smell of incense or candle wax create a door to your inner wisdom.

6. Now observe how you feel. Do you have any sensations? Or emotions? Be aware of how you respond to this place of power. Are particular parts of your body stimulated, animated, or calmed by this spot? Or by the synergy of this sacred site with your question? Do you feel a pulse of energy? If so, where in your body? Give your query over to this place of power and notice what happens as you continue to meditate.

7. After meditating for five to ten minutes, repeat your question silently to yourself.

8. Meditate for a few more minutes if you have yet to receive an oracle.

9. Interpret your divination, possibly with the help of free association (p. 18).

10. Thank the sacred site for its wisdom.

CONTINUING THE JOURNEY

Your experience with the **Connecting to Source** oracle depends largely on which type of sacred site you've selected. At a place of personal power, your experience will probably involve emotional responses to your query, since these are sites that hold important memories for you. At a church or synagogue, your divinatory experience will be strengthened by the religious symbols surrounding you as well as the atmosphere created by the many sacred events that have taken place in that particular building.

Where ley lines cross and form the third type of sacred site, they create vortices of qi-like energy. The effect of this kind of holy place will depend on the variety of energy located there and your openness to it. During my trip to England in 1997, for instance, I experienced energies that affected me in very different ways.

I traveled to England as a skeptic. I believed that the earth was sacred, but that no single place was any more sacred than another, except for the associations we bring to it. But an unforgettable experience changed my mind, and it happened in the Cotswolds, an area of England whose name translates into modern English as "God's high open land."

One evening, my family and I ended up at the Rollright Stones, one of the many stone circles that dot the countryside in that part of southern England. A number of people were at the site when we arrived, including four New Age folks with didjeridus. I stopped to ask them about the myths surrounding the place, and after listening to the most gregarious man in the group, I began to reply, but then stopped in midsentence, surprised by a sudden tingling in my heels. It seemed to flow from the earth into the bottom of my feet and then upward into my ankles, a sensation similar to the "pins and needles" you experience when an arm, leg, or foot has "fallen asleep" and finally begins to regain feeling.

This was completely unexpected. In fact, it was a shock—both literally and figuratively. I wasn't tuning into the earth, meditating, or trying to reach an altered state of consciousness; I was having a pleasant conversation in a normal state of mind. When I said something about the prickling sensation, the young man with the didjeridu acknowledged that he had felt it, too. That surprised me even more, for he confirmed what I might have brushed off as a trick of my vivid imagination.

My understanding of sacred sites was changed forever. From one moment to the next, the Rollright Stones had jolted my awareness awake, and I realized that such sacred sites were charged with energies. As I continued my travels, I disovered that each stone circle emanated a different "frequency" that I "received" in one or more of my chakras. At Avebury, it was my second chakra, since it was the site for celebrating the ancient Goddess's sexuality, and at Stonehenge, the energy was linked to both the first and fifth chakras.

Places of power like these ancient stone circles and monuments in England, Scotland, and Ireland exist all over the world, but they're not always distinguished by human-made earthworks. In North America, pictographs and petroglyphs line the rock canyons of the West at some holy sites, but many of our continent's sacred locations are mountains, lakes, caves, or unusual rock formations, to name just a few examples. As a result, they don't always bear human-made signs of their significance.

One way to locate such sites is through their names. This is easier to manage in Europe since, prior to Christian times, sacred sites were associated with deities who could aid petitioners: *genii loci* in Latin or *daemons* in Greek.[50] Some of these guardian spirits were assimilated into the Christian tradition as saints by early Church fathers, while others were excluded as devils. As a result, today's geographical names often point to sacred sites, either by stipulating a "demon's" domain or by designating a saint's.

If you're visiting a sacred site, no matter where in the world you are, remember that it's important to discover whether it's open to people who aren't native to the region, and whether there are any taboos concerning it. We all need to approach such places in a respectful manner, realizing that we're treading on holy ground.

SMUDGING

BURNING CONFUSION AWAY

› ADVANCED ‹

All over the world people purify themselves and their surroundings in order to prepare for sacred experiences, including ritual, divination, meditation, healing, chanting, and drumming. Many traditional Native Americans smudge for this reason. From the Omàmiwininì (Algonquins) on the East Coast to the Chumash on the West Coast, they burn sacred herbs—often sage, cedar, and sweetgrass—to cleanse all participants in body, mind, and spirit prior to their ceremonies.[K] The Roman Catholic Church uses incense for a similar purpose, while Orthodox Judaism requires its believers under certain circumstances to bathe in a *mikveh*—a bath or pool—in order to become ritually pure.

In Japanese Shinto temples, there are several purification practices prior to any ceremony. They begin with rinsing hands and mouth with water, continue with ringing a bell, and finally end with participating in the *Shubatsu* ritual, during which a priest waves a *harai-gushi* wand (or *õnusa*) over participants: This wand has strips of paper at its end, which sweep away any negativity participants might bring into the temple.[51] In each of these religions, such cleansing opens a space for the sacred to enter and allows a person to become more fully present—exactly what you need for a successful divination.

burning confusion away:
as smoke washes over your body,
all unnecessary thoughts,
sensations, and feelings blow away,
so you can attend to your issue
without their interference.

WHERE — Anywhere fireproof

WHEN — Anytime

HOW — Sitting or standing

TOOLS — A smudge stick or incense

A fireproof area, in your house or elsewhere, for instance, a fireproof kitchen counter or hearth

A fireproof container

I've adapted smudging as a divination method so that you can settle into an oracular mind-set and get in touch with your deeper knowing. Purifying yourself can lighten your mood, too, since it ritualizes the act of eliminating extraneous thoughts or feelings concerning your query. The symbolism of cleansing yourself of these interfering emotions will also help you achieve a more positive mood. This is significant, because science has demonstrated that positive emotions, such as tranquility, joy, and love, facilitate creative insights.[A]

Cat Criger, Aboriginal elder-in-residence at the University of Toronto, suggests that you use a wooden match to light your smudge stick, following the traditional American Indian practice. He also states that the sacred herbs that you use need to be treated with reverence. Do this by storing them in an honored place. You should also dispose of the ashes outdoors by leaving them on the earth.[K] The technique **Burning Your Confusion Away** will appeal most to people who enjoy open-ended oracles.

STEPS

1. Formulate your question (p. 12).

2. Decide on a fireproof location where you can safely smudge.

3. Collect your tools.

4. Ground and center (p. 15). Let your meditation create a space separate from your everyday life and a mind-set free of your ordinary, analytical thinking.

5. Light your smudge stick or piece of incense in the fireproof area. As you do so, remind yourself of your query.

6. When your incense or smudge stick is burning well, put out the flame by gently blowing on it over the fireproof container. The incense or smudge stick will smolder, giving off smoke.

7. Place your hands in the smoke and make motions that imitate washing them. Then sweep the smoke up over your head and shoulders with your hands, a fan, or a feather. Start at your head

and move downward, letting the smoke cleanse your entire aura of any extraneous thoughts or feelings.

8. As the fragrant smoke washes over your body, imagine that it carries away anything that might block your divination, so that you can welcome a response to your query. Notice how the room goes from smoky to clear, just as your thinking moves toward clarity concerning your issue. Let this change open a free space in your mind, allowing it to be receptive to new ideas.

9. Place your smudge stick in the fireproof container or take it outside and let it go out naturally.

10. Now meditate or sit in silence with your question for ten minutes at most. You've prepared the ground for guidance by smudging the area and inviting clarity: Now simply remain open to the inner wisdom you will receive.

11. Identify and interpret the guidance you've gained, possibly with the help of free association (p. 18).

12. Thank the smudge or incense for your oracle.

CONTINUING THE JOURNEY

In good weather, it's practical to undertake **Smudging** oracles outside, where you can leave the smudge stick at the edge of your yard and eventually scatter the ashes there. If you perform this divination inside, your kitchen offers the best setting. Here, you can light your smudge stick or incense over the sink or stove and turn on your hood, if you have one, for sufficient ventilation.

It's best to meditate after smudging, as the steps above suggest, remembering your oracular question from time to time as you do so. Sometimes an answer will come during your smudging, but often you'll get an inkling of your inner guidance once you've finished, while you're sitting in silence. You might need to revisit this practice—sometimes a number of times over the following days—in order to quiet your surface mind enough to get in touch with your deepest wisdom.

TREES

TAPROOT TO WITHIN

› ADVANCED ‹

As the largest plant on Earth, the tree has fascinated humans from the beginning of time. It has fed us with its fruits, provided us with shelter and shade, and has kept us warm by giving us wood for burning. Trees also resemble us in many ways, a fact that explains the ease with which we can communicate with them. As Shug tells Celie in Alice Walker's *The Color Purple*, "Everything want to be loved. Us sing and dance, make faces and give flower bouquets, trying to be loved. You ever notice that trees do everything to git attention we do, except walk?"

Many traditions worldwide have considered trees sacred. In the East, Hinduism and Buddhism still revere *yakshas* and *yakshis*, ancient earth divinities linked with trees. In Mesopotamia, the sacred tree was associated with the Goddess Inanna and her successor Ishtar and eventually came down to us in the Bible as the Tree of Life. And the Celts venerated all trees as holy; in fact, our superstition of "knocking on wood" probably stems from the Celts, for whom reverently touching trees brought wisdom, protection, and the luck we expect from rapping on the closest wooden table.[52]

Given this background, it shouldn't surprise us to discover that trees have offered people a wonderful source for oracles. In fact, *xylomancy* was the ancient divination method of reading twigs that had fallen in your path—a method that still exists in eastern Croatia today—while *dendromancy* burned oak or mistletoe and observed the patterns made by the resulting smoke.[53] Today, lots of people have "favorite" trees; that is, they find that certain trees really resonate with

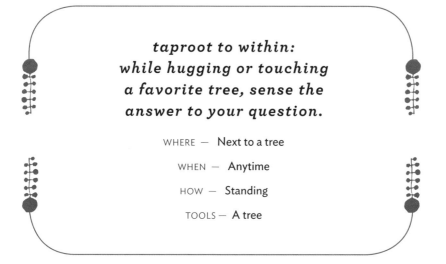

taproot to within:
while hugging or touching
a favorite tree, sense the
answer to your question.

WHERE — Next to a tree

WHEN — Anytime

HOW — Standing

TOOLS — A tree

them. Since love is one of the emotions that prime us for divination, this oracular method takes our love of such trees as the starting point for an oracle.

The best way to begin a tree divination is by befriending a tree that grows near your house. Although most trees welcome your questions, if you have an ongoing relationship with one, it will be more likely to respond to your divination needs. One way to cultivate such connections is to leave an offering of loose tobacco or cornmeal. This is an American Indian custom, and it's something that trees seem to appreciate.

By definition, a **Tree** oracle will take you outside. This is a good thing, since neuroscientists indicate that the ideal environments for awakening your inner guidance are "open, airy, soft, rounded, and calm" surroundings, a good description of most of nature. Such an expansive setting will allow your mind to expand as well, permitting new thoughts to arise.[A]

Like all divinations in *The World Is Your Oracle*, a Tree oracle takes for granted that humans are an integral part of the interdependent web of all existence. Contemporary science is also examining this idea; take, for instance, the Gaia theory, which argues that Earth is a synergistic, self-regulating, complex system that includes all of the flora and fauna that live upon it.[54] There is an underlying reality that unifies all of life, what the Chinese call the *Tao*: This means that everything is connected—including you and your favorite tree.

STEPS

1. Formulate your question (p. 12).

2. Locate your divinatory tree and acknowledge it as your source of guidance.

3. Ground and center near the tree (p. 15). Let your meditation create a space separate from your everyday life and a mind-set free of your ordinary, analytical thinking.

4. Greet the tree by reciting poetry, singing, or simply by saying, "Hello."

5. Embrace the tree. Press your forehead or the palms of your hands against its bark and then tell it your question mind-to-mind.

6. Sense the tree's reply for up to ten minutes. Feel the stability of its roots under your feet, sending a taproot into the earth's wisdom. Feel the sap rising in answer to your presence, filling you with new ideas. Stroke the bark, hold on to a branch, or caress one of the tree's leaves, all the time centering your attention on the tree's response to you. While you're communing with your tree, perhaps an insect will run across your hand or a bird will sing above you. Any of these could answer your question. Perhaps the tree will drop a twig, nut, or fruit; perhaps it will rustle in a telling way; or it may just give you a feeling that nudges you toward more openness to your quandary.

7. Interpret the outcome, perhaps with the help of free association (p. 18).

8. Thank your chosen tree for your oracle.

CONTINUING THE JOURNEY

If you're a kinesthetic diviner, you will probably feel something—either a physical sensation or an emotion—as your answer. But sometimes the tree's response will come when a fruit, stick, or leaf drops. It's also possible that, while you're waiting, something will catch your attention as you embrace your oracular tree. Perhaps a car will drive by with its windows open, blaring the answer to your question on its radio. Or you'll notice a cloud that looks like a particular animal or some other identifiable object, indicating a symbolic response to your query. As with all divinatory practices, the more you're open to the universe, the more it will respond.

WALKING
ZEN CONCENTRATION WALK

› ADVANCED ‹

Walking plays an important role in many spiritual traditions. Within Taoism, a variety of walking qigong practices have existed for centuries, the most recent form invented in the 1950s by Guo Lin as a method for healing cancer.[55] Buddhists also undertake a number of walking meditations; in fact, according to some sources, the Buddha himself taught a walking meditation to his followers.[56] In Japan, members of this religion engage in a meditative practice called the Zen walk, while *Vipassana* adherents in other parts of the world walk as well as sit while meditating.[D] Pagans experience the sacredness of the earth as they hike through forests, deserts, and savannahs, or stroll along lakes and oceans.

In addition to these practices, pilgrimage represents a significant aspect of the major religions of the world. In Islam, every Muslim must undertake the *hajj*, or sacred journey to Mecca, at least once during their lifetime (unless seriously ill). Within Hinduism and Buddhism, pilgrims visit sacred temples and shrines, as well as holy mountains, stones, and trees, especially the Bodhi Tree, where the Buddha attained enlightenment. Christians flock to many pilgrimage sites in Europe as well as to Guadalupe's shrine in Mexico City and, of course, Jerusalem and Bethlehem in the Holy Land. In this divination practice, I adapted a Japanese walking meditation as a means of accessing your innermost thoughts.

zen concentration walk:
while thinking about your question
as if it were a koan, walk mindfully to
experience your reality as it truly is.

WHERE — Preferably outside

WHEN — Anytime

HOW — Walking

TOOLS — A path

Within Japanese Zen Buddhism, monks practice *kinhin*, a type of concentration meditation. The meditator walks slowly with hands crossed tightly at the chest, all the while concentrating on a koan, a seemingly nonsensical problem meant to challenge the mind to see reality as it truly is. In Zen, as in this divination technique (in a more limited way), the goal is "the sudden flashing into consciousness of a new truth hitherto undreamed of." This is how D. T. Suzuki defines *satori*, or sudden enlightenment—the ultimate objective of Zen Buddhism.

In many ways, oracular queries resemble koans, since confusion usually leads to the need for divination as well as the hope for clarity and greater insight. Similarly, a koan initially appears illogical or paradoxical in order to open up a person's view to a wider and wiser perspective. In this oracular method, your divinatory question takes the place of the traditional koan. The **Zen Concentration Walk** is designed to free you from your emotional or intellectual attachments to specific ways of viewing your concern. As with other forms of meditation, it will ultimately lead to a greater lucidity regarding your issue.

STEPS

1. Find a walking path with a relatively flat surface that is at least thirty to forty feet (9 to 12 m) long.

2. Formulate your question (p. 12).

3. Ground and center (p. 15). Let your meditation create a space separate from your everyday life and a mind-set free of your ordinary, analytical thinking.

4. Cross your hands tightly across your chest and restate your query in your mind.

5. Walk slowly and deliberately, all the while concentrating on your question. Feel into your query from as many perspectives as possible, as if you were rolling it around in your hand to experience it from different angles. From one angle, it may feel shiny and new; from another, tarnished and dull. Make a note of these

differences. Focus on your question and notice all of its ins and outs.

6. Sense how your body responds to your question. Attune yourself to the steady pace at which you're walking, synchronizing your thinking with each stride. Let the repetitive cadence of your footsteps take you to fresh possibilities about your issue.

7. If your mind wanders from your question, watch the direction in which it moves. For example, does this supposed distraction inform you of blocks to your understanding? Does it lead you to deeper insights into your question? Once you've answered these questions, gently return to concentrating on your query.

8. If your guidance hasn't arrived after ten to fifteen minutes, meditate while seated for another few minutes.

9. Take note of your divinatory outcome. What guidance did your oracle offer you?

10. Interpret your oracle, using free association (p. 18), if necessary, to unlock its secrets.

11. Thank your feet for your oracle.

CONTINUING THE JOURNEY

Many people tend to stop their meditation if a new perception occurs while walking. In my experience, however, if you return to your oracular question, other insights often follow. So try not to dwell on the new understandings as they arise, unless you know you'll forget them. Just note what you've learned, then go back to thinking about your question.

Also, remember that this type of open-ended oracle has its own timetable. Your guidance may arrive while you meditate, just after you finish, or even days or weeks later. In fact, if you're dealing with a particularly ingrained problem, you may need to undertake more than one walking meditation in order to dislodge your fixed beliefs or entrenched feelings and receive the guidance you seek.

WORKS FREQUENTLY CITED

[A] Kounios, John, and Mark Beeman. *The Eureka Factor: Aha Moments, Creative Insight, and the Brain*. New York: Random House, 2015.

[B] Cavendish, Richard, ed. *Man, Myth and Magic: The Illustrated Encyclopedia of Mythology, Religion, and the Unknown*. New York: Marshall Cavendish, 1995.

[C] Bluestone, Sarvananda. *How to Read Signs and Omens in Everyday Life*. Rochester, VT: Destiny Books, 2002.

[D] Earheart, H. Byron, ed. *Religious Traditions of the World: A Journey through Africa, North America, Mesoamerica, Judaism, Christianity, Islam, Hinduism, Buddhism, China, and Japan*. San Francisco: HarperOne, 1992.

[E] Woolfolk, Joanna Martine. *The Only Astrology Book You'll Ever Need*. Lanham, MD: Scarborough House Publishers, 1982.

[F] Roche, Lorin. *The Radiance Sutras: 112 Gateways to the Yoga of Wonder and Delight*. Boulder, CO: Sounds True, 2014.

[G] Skafte, Dianne. *Listening to the Oracle: The Ancient Art of Finding Guidance in the Signs and Symbols All Around Us*. San Francisco: HarperSanFrancisco, 1997.

[H] Buckland, Raymond. *The Fortune-Telling Book: The Encyclopedia of Divination and Soothsaying*. Canton, MI: Visible Ink Press, 2004.

[I] Baldwin, Christina. *Life's Companion: Journal Writing as a Spiritual Quest*. New York: Bantam Books, 1990.

[J] Hirschi, Gertrud. *Mudras: Yoga in Your Hands*. San Francisco: Weiser Books, 2000.

[K] Charleyboy, Lisa. "The Ancient Art of Smudging." *Spirituality & Health*, November/December 2012.

REFERENCES

Almaas, A. H. *Spacecruiser Inquiry: True Guidance for the Inner Journey*. Boston: Shambhala Publications, 2002.

Baraz, James, and Shoshana Alexander. *Awakening Joy: 10 Steps That Will Put You on the Road to Real Happiness*. New York: Bantam Books, 2010.

Bonheim, Jalaja. *The Hunger for Ecstasy: Fulfilling the Soul's Need for Passion and Intimacy*. Emmaus, PA: Rodale Press, 2001.

Cameron, Julia. *The Artist's Way: A Spiritual Path to Higher Creativity*. New York: Tarcher/Putnam Books, 1992.

de Bono, Edward. *New Think: The Use of Lateral Thinking*. London: Jonathan Cape, 1967.

de Bono, Edward. "Lateral Thinking," http://www.edwdebono.com/lateral.htm.

Gaynor, Mitchell L. *The Healing Power of Sound: Recovery from Life-Threatening Illness Using Sound, Voice, and Music*. Boston: Shambhala Publications, 2002.

Harner, Michael. *The Way of the Shaman: A Guide to Power and Healing*. New York: Harper & Row, 1980.

Hay, Louise. *Heal Your Body*. Hay House, 1984.

Richards, Mary Caroline. *Centering in Pottery, Poetry, and the Person*. Middletown, CT: Wesleyan University Press, 1964.

Suzuki, D. T. *An Introduction to Zen Buddhism*. New York: Grove Press, 1964.

ENDNOTES

[1] "Capitalizing on Complexity: Insights from the Global Chief Executive Officer Study," IBM (2010), accessed August 2, 2015, http://public.dhe.ibm.com/common/ssi/ecm/gb/en/gbe03297usen/GBE03297USEN.PDF, p. 8.

[2] Helen Phillips, "Mind Fiction: Why Your Brain Tells Tall Tales," *New Scientist* (October 4, 2006).

[3] Rue Anne Hass, *This Is Where I Stand* (Starseed Publications, 2008).

[4] Maharaji, subsequently used as a title for one of his books.

[5] My friend Lorin Roche describes this process for meditation in *The Radiance Sutras: 112 Gateways to the Yoga of Wonder and Delight* (Boulder, CO: Sounds True, 2014). He writes, "An overall skill of meditation is allowing each surprising moment of your experience to invoke just the right quality of engagement" (p. 238). The same is true for divination.

[6] As reported by Christopher Bergland, "Alpha Brain Waves Boost Creativity and Reduce Depression." *Psychology Today*, (April 17, 2015), accessed September 13, 2015, https://www.psychologytoday.com/blog/the-athletes-way/201504/alpha-brain-waves-boost-creativity-and-reduce-depression.

[7] Consistent rhythmic stimuli, like those of a fast-beating drum or rattle, can synchronize the brain's waves to those same rhythms, inducing a deeply relaxing trance. This is called brain wave entrainment.

[8] Kate Douglas, "Subconscious: The Other You," *New Scientist* 196 (December 1, 2007): 42–46.

[9] John Robinson, *Archaeologica Graeca* (London: R. Phillips, 1807), 281.

[10] Harry Mountain, *The Celtic Encyclopedia*, Vol. 1 (Upublish.com, 1998), p. 267. Available on Google Books: https://books.google.com/books?id=LTbc1GIAwcIC. Once in preview mode, search for "Celtic ashes divination" within the book.

[11] Paul Hyer and Sechin Jagchid, *A Mongolian Living Buddha: A Biography of the Kanjurwa Khutughtu* (Albany, NY: State University of New York Press, 1983), 119.

[12] Madam Juno, *The Gypsy Queen Dream Book and Fortune Teller* (Pymble, Australia: Obscure Press, 2005), 15.

[13] Ellen Russell Emerson, *Indian Myths: or Legends, Traditions, and Symbols of the Aborigines of America* (Boston: Houghton Mifflin, 1885), 110.

[14] See Joshua Trachtenberg, *Jewish Magic and Superstition: A Study in Folk Religion* (Forgotten Books, originally published in 1939, republished by Google's Forgotten Books, https://books.google.com/books/about/Jewish_Magic_and_Superstition.html?id=6YC5BkVrJo4C, 214–19; Dorje Tseten, "Tibetan Art of Divination," *Tibetan Bulletin* (March-April 1995), http://tibetanaltar.blogspot.com/2010/09/methods-of-tibetan-divination.html; "How to Read Divination Signs from Candle–Burning: Ceromancy in Hoodoo Candle Magic," *Candle Magic in the Hoodoo Rootwork Tradition*, http://www.luckymojo.com/candlemagic.html and http://www.luckymojo.com/candlemagicdivination.html.

[15] Phillip Vandenberg, *Mysteries of the Oracles: The Last Secrets of Antiquity* (New York: Tauris Parke Paperbacks, 2007), 233. You can find this in Herodotus's *Histories*, edited by A. D. Godley (London: Heinemann: 1920), 2:141.

[16] John Nelson, *The Magic Mirror: Divination through the Ancient Art of Scrying* (Charlottesville, VA: Hampton Roads Publishing Company, 2007), 5-9.

[17] Carl Huffman, "Pythagoras," *The Stanford Encyclopedia of Philosophy*, (fall 2011 edition), edited by Edward N. Zalta, http://plato.stanford.edu/entries/pythagoras/#LifWor; Carl G. Jung, "Synchronicity: An Acausal

Connecting Principle," in *Collected Works of C.G. Jung*, 2nd ed., vol. 8 (Princeton: Bollingen Series: 1969), 456ff.

[18] Zhaawano Giizhik, "The Universe of the Ojibwe/Anishinaabeg: A Glossary," https://www.yumpu.com/en/document/view/37335042. p. 4.

[19] A shamanic journey can also be undertaken to the "upper world," where you meet and talk with a spiritual teacher, most often in human form. The technique described here is journeying to the lower world.

[20] Although I thought I created this divination method, I'm sure it must have been inspired by Sarvananda Bluestone's "Reflect Yourself in the Sky" exercise in *How to Read Signs and Omens in Everyday Life* (Rochester, VT: Destiny Books, 2002, 46–47), since it is very similar.

[21] Layne Redmond, *When the Drummers were Women: A Spiritual History of Rhythm* (New York: Three Rivers Press, 1997), 47.

[22] In Robert Lawrence Friedman, *The Healing Power of the Drum* (Reno, NV: White Cliffs, 2000). See also Michael Winkelman, *Shamanism: The Neural Ecology of Consciousness and Healing* (Westport, CT: Bergin & Garvey, 2000).

[23] See Mitchell L. Gaynor, M.D., *Sounds of Healing: A Physician Reveals the Therapeutic Power of Sound, Voice and Music* (New York: Broadway Books, 1999).

[24] Gerina Dunwich, *Candlelight Spells: The Modern Witch's Book of Spellcasting, Feasting, and Healing* (Secaucus, NJ: Citadel Press, 1988), 51.

[25] David Mager, "Brain Wave Entrainment," *Huffington Post* (October 24, 2013), accessed September 19, 2015, http://www.huffingtonpost.com/david-mager/brain-wave-entrainment_b_4142898.html.

[26] See Joseph Schorr, *Psychotherapy Through Imagery* (NY: Intercontinental Medical Book Corp., 1974).

[27] Robert Graves, *Greek Myths, Revised Edition*, vol. 1 (London: Penguin Books, 1960), 181.

[28] André Caquot, "La Divination dans l'ancien Israel," in André Caquot and Marcel Leibovici, eds., *La Divination*, vol. 2 (Paris: Presse Universitaires de France, 1968), 102. We find this passage in II Samuel 5: 22–25. In various versions of the Bible, the trees are identified as mulberry, balsam, or poplar.

[29] Jamie Sams, "Sacred Medicine: Native North-American Divination Systems," in John Matthews, ed., *The World Atlas of Divination: The Systems, Where they Originate, How They Work* (Boston: Little Brown, 1992), 111.

[30] Robert Sutherland Tattray, *Religion and Art in Ashanti* (Oxford: Clarendon Press, 1927), 44–45.

[31] Rob Margetta, "What Happens When 'Aha' Strikes," *National Science Foundation* (August 3, 2015), accessed August 15, 2015, http://www.nsf.gov/discoveries/disc_summ.jsp?cntn_id=135833.

[32] William Brede Kristensen, *The Meaning of Religion: Lectures in the Phenomenology of Religion* (The Hague, Netherlands: Martinus Nijhoff, 1960), 104.

[33] John Manas, *Divination Ancient and Modern: An Historical, Archaeological and Philosophical Approach to Seership and Christian Religion* (Whitefish, MT: Kessinger Publishing, 2004), 67.

[34] "Brainwaves—And What They Represent," *Brainwaves and Consciousness*, accessed October 3, 2015, http://www.hirnwellen-und-bewusstsein.de/brainwaves_1.html.

[35] Discovering your physical anchor is a technique that I learned in a Reclaiming workshop with Rose May Dance. I've adapted it for use in **Body Sense**. Rene Peace led me through a body trance that inspired this divination technique. I've fleshed it out for use as an oracular tool.

36 See Starhawk, *The Spiral Dance: A Rebirth of the Ancient Religion of the Goddess* (San Francisco: Harper & Row, 1979), 22–24.

37 Colin Blakemore and Shelia Jennett, "Hands" and "Feet," *Oxford Companion to the Body* (Oxford: Oxford University Press, 2001).

38 I learned about *qi* and its relationship to the chakra system from Tricia Yu, who founded the Tai Chi Center in Madison.

39 Duffi McDermott, "Foot and Hand Chakras," http://heartpsychic.blogspot.com/2008/07/foot-and-hand-chakras.html, accessed October 17, 2016; "Hindu Culture," http://mailerindia.com/hindu/veda/index.php?hculture, accessed October 17, 2016.

40 Francesca Rochberg, *The Heavenly Writing: Divination, Horoscopy, and Astronomy in Mesopotamian Culture* (Cambridge: Cambridge University Press, 2004), 1–2.

41 Barbara Lesko, *The Great Goddesses of Egypt* (Norman, OK: University of Oklahoma Press, 1999), 374.

42 Automatic Writing," *New World Encyclopedia*, http://www.newworldencyclopedia.org/entry/Automatic_writing#Automatic_Writing_and_the_Surrealists.

43 Psychologist Mihaly Czikszentmihalyi invented the concept of "flow" as I'm using it here. It refers to "a state of concentration so focused that it amounts to absolute absorption in an activity." As quoted in Charlene Belitz and Meg Lundstrom, *The Power of Flow: Practical Ways to Transform Your Life with Meaningful Coincidence* (New York: Three Rivers Press, 1998), 2.

44 As quoted in Christina Baldwin, *Life's Companion: Journal Writing as a Spiritual Quest* (New York: Bantam Books, 1990), 303.

45 The first of these studies was done by Dr. Herbert Benson and reported in the book he wrote with Miriam Klipper, *The Relaxation Response* (New York: William Morrow, 1975).

46 Jennifer Reis, "Mudra Yoga," *Kripalu Newsletter*, accessed May 17, 2016, https://kripalu.org/resources/mudra-yoga.

47 See Jemima Montagu, *The Surrealists: Revolutionaries in Art and Writing 1919-1935* (London: Tate Publications, 2002).

48 For more interpretive ideas, see Samantha Snyder, "Doodle Art Alley," http://www.doodle-art-alley.com/why-doodle.html or Helen South, "Drawing/Sketching," http://drawsketch.about.com/cs/tipsandideas/a/doodle_2.htm.

49 See Robert Graves, *Greek Myths, Revised Edition* (London: Penguin Books, 1960).

50 While our English word *demon* derives from the Greek *daemon*, the two have nothing in common. A *daemon* was a largely beneficent spirit who was associated with and guarded a sacred site. Many were heroes in life and continued their role as protector after death.

51 Mogi Sadasumi, "Shubatsu," *Encyclopedia of Shinto*. Go to http://k-amc.kokugakuin.ac.jp/DM/dbTop.do?class_name=col_eos and search "Shubatsu."

52 D. J. Conway, *Celtic Magic* (St. Paul, MN: Llewellyn Publications, 1990), 158.

53 See Clifford Pickover, *Dreaming the Future: The Fantastic Story of Prediction* (Amherst, NY: Prometheus Books, 2001), 137, 182.

54 See James Lovelock, *Gaia: A New Look at Life on Earth*, 2nd ed. (Oxford: Oxford University Press, 2016).

55 David Palmer, *Qigong Fever: Body, Science, and Utopia in China* (New York: Columbia University Press, 2007).

56 John Bowker, *The Oxford Dictionary of World Religions* (New York: Oxford University Press, 1999), 224; Sayadaw U. Silananda, "The Benefits of Walking Meditation," *Bodhi Leaves* No. B 137 (Kandy, Sri Lanka: Buddhist Publication Society, 1995).

RESOURCES

Here are some resources I turn to when performing **Chanting, Drumming, Divine Inspiration,** or **Creatures** oracles.

chanting and other music

If you wish to sing one of the sacred songs I've suggested for a **Chanting** oracle, you can find it in the books listed below.

ATHEIST

Blood, Peter, and Annie Patterson, eds. *Rise Up Singing: The Group Singing Songbook.* Bethlehem, PA: A Sing Out! Publication, 1988.

BUDDHIST

Dances of Universal Peace, vol. 2. Seattle: PeaceWorks, 1982, p. 16.

HINDU

Dances of Universal Peace, vol. 3. Seattle: PeaceWorks, 1985, p. 9.

MUSLIM

Lewis, Samuel L. *Original Dances of Murshid Samuel L. Lewis* Seattle: PeaceWorks, 1990.

"OM TARA"

Chants for the Queen of Heaven is available from my website, www.mamasminstrel.net.

Kealoha, Anna, ed. *Songs of the Earth: Music of the Earth.* Berkeley, CA: Celestial Arts, 1989, p. 30.

PAGAN, WICCAN, OR NATIVE AMERICAN

Marks, Kate, ed. *Circle of Song: Songs, Chants, and Dances for Ritual and Celebration.* Lenox, MA: Full Circle Press, 1993.

Middleton, Julie Forest, ed. *Songs for Earthlings: A Green Spirituality Songbook.* Philadelphia: Emerald Earth Publishing, 1998. You can contact Julie at P.O. Box 4326, Philadelphia, PA 19118.

drumming

You can buy recordings of drumming through the Foundation for Shamanic Studies at http://www.shamanism.org/products/audio.html#1.

Information about Siberian drumming is in Nicholas Breeze Wood, "Soul Drum," http://www.3worlds.co.uk/Articles/The-Soul-of-the-shaman.pdf.

gods, goddesses, saints, and power animals

If you need to research Gods, Goddesses, saints, or animal spirits with specific areas of expertise, here are some books that may be of use.

Andrews, Ted. *Animal-Speak: The Spiritual and Magical Powers of Creatures Great and Small.* St. Paul, MN: Llewellyn Publications, 1996.

Carr-Gomm, Philip, and Stephanie Carr-Gomm. *The Druid Animal Oracle: Working with the Sacred Animals of the Druid Tradition.* New York: Simon & Schuster, 1994.

Clark, Tess, Elizabeth Hallam, and Cecilia Walters. *Saints: Who They Are and How They Help You.* New York: Simon & Schuster, 1994.

Jordan, Michael. *Encyclopedia of Gods: Over Twenty-Five Hundred Deities of the World.* New York: Facts on File, 1993.

Monaghan, Patricia. *Encyclopedia of Goddesses and Heroines.* Novato, CA: New World Library, 2014.

Sams, Jamie, and David Carson. *Medicine Cards: The Discovery of Power through the Ways of Animals.* Santa Fe, NM: Bear & Company, 1988.

birds, animals, and insects

Although I have used my own insight into birds, animals, and insects to compile associations, I gathered much of my information from the following:

Andrews, Ted. *Animal-Speak: The Spiritual and Magical Powers of Creatures Great and Small*. St. Paul, MN: Llewellyn Publications, 1996.

———. *Animal-Wise*. Jackson, TN: Dragonhawk Publishing, 1999.

Carr-Gomm, Philip, and Stephanie Carr-Gomm. *The Druid Animal Oracle: Working with the Sacred Animals of the Druid Tradition*. New York: Simon & Schuster, 1994.

Collins, Henry Hill Jr. *The Complete Field Guide to American Wildlife*. New York: Harper & Brothers, 1959.

Conway, D. J. *Animal Magick*. Saint Paul, MN: Llewellyn Publications, 1995.

Sams, Jamie, and David Carson. *Medicine Cards: The Discovery of Power through the Ways of Animals*. Santa Fe, NM: Bear & Company, 1988.

INDEX

APPENDIX

creatures: guidance from the wild

These tables list bugs, animals, and birds common to several North American regions. Some shy or rare creatures might be recognized only through signs of their presence, like footprints, scent (of a skunk, for instance), scat, or other indications that they've been in the area. You may also see a photo or picture of an animal, bird, or insect. Just stay open to the moment, and you'll know which critter is helping you.

ASSOCIATIONS WITH COMMON NORTH AMERICAN BUGS

BUG	ASSOCIATIONS	PERSONAL MEANINGS
Ant	Industriousness, working with others, order, drudgery	
Bee	Sweetness of life, being busy, stinging, community	
Beetle	Protection, having a hard shell, hidden wings, faerie realm	
Butterfly, moth	Transmutation, fragile beauty, the soul, night-time magic	
Cockroach	Survival, scavenging, adaptability, disgust	
Cricket	Good luck, good cheer, easy living, long antennae	
Dragonfly	Magic, illusions, instantaneous change of direction	
Fly	Health issues, pest, transforming decay, seeing many ways	
Grasshopper	Leaping, escaping, finding warmth and light, laziness	
Ladybug	Good luck, happiness, well-being, fulfillment of wishes	
Mosquito	Annoyance, blood, itching, stagnant water (where they breed)	
Spider	Creativity, weaving, capturing what we want, poison	
Wasp	Interpersonal nastiness, paralysis, aggression	

ASSOCIATIONS WITH COMMON NORTH AMERICAN ANIMALS

ANIMAL	ASSOCIATIONS	PERSONAL MEANINGS
Bat	Night vision, seeing through illusion, intuition, transformation	
Bear	Primal power, hibernation	
Chipmunk	Scavenging, storing reserves, scurrying, attention to detail	
Cow	Nurturing, rumination, slow movement	
Deer	Gentleness, grace, innocence, purity	
Frog	Metamorphosis, adaptability, primeval waters, prince in disguise	
Horse	Travel, power, freedom, sexual strength (stallion), wildness	
Lizard	Intuition, dreams, escape from danger	
Mouse	Awareness, cowardice, hoarding, tidiness, pestilence	
Rabbit	Fertility, fear	
Raccoon	Dexterity, disguises, resourcefulness	
Rat	Shrewdness, pest, scoundrel	
Skunk	Defense, unpleasant to be around, demanding respect	
Snake	Nonpoisonous: rebirth, casting off the old, cleverness Poisonous: poisonous thoughts, danger, deceit, vengeance	
Squirrel	Preparedness (for winter), scattered activity, forgetfulness	
Turtle	At home everywhere, slow and steady progress, self-protection	
Woodchuck	The underworld, winter or spring (seeing its shadow)	

ASSOCIATIONS WITH COMMON NORTH AMERICAN BIRDS

BIRD	ASSOCIATIONS	PERSONAL MEANINGS
Blue jay	Power, intelligence, showiness, bullying	
Cardinal	Flamboyance, renewed vitality, feminine mysteries	
Chickadee	Cheerfulness, tameness, charm	
Chicken	Fertility, sacrifice, grounded mind, sustenance, fear	
Crow	Wiliness, nuisance, the supernatural, shape-shifting, death	
Duck	Emotional intelligence, emotional vulnerability (ducklings)	
Goldfinch	Joy, liveliness, sunshine	
Goose	Travel, fidelity, "wild goose chase"	
Grackle	Noisy chattering, emotions coloring thinking process	
Gull	Crossing boundaries, nuisance, dumpster diving	
Hawk	Boldness, clear-sightedness, seizing opportunities	
House sparrow	Commonness, domesticity, fertility, annoyance	
Hummingbird	Joy and sweetness, beauty, preciousness, amazement	
Mourning dove	Peace, grieving, spirit	
Pigeon	Fertility, street wisdom, homing instinct, dirtiness	
Robin	New beginnings, cheerfulness, harbinger of spring	
Rooster	Cockiness, aggression, noisiness, calling attention to oneself	
Starling	Community, talkativeness, mob behavior, imitation	
Swallow	Master of the air, herald of summer, weak grounding	
Woodpecker	Rhythm, perserverance, resourcefulness	

numbers: numerical wisdom

You may have personal associations with some of these numbers. When performing a divination, these will almost always outweigh more general cultural connotations.

NUMERICAL ASSOCIATIONS

NUMBER	ASSOCIATIONS	PERSONAL MEANINGS
0	The void, God as source, Goddess' yoni, cosmic egg, boundlessness, absence of all quantity or quality	
1	Beginning, essence, unity, seed, individuality, will, divine spark, independence, one world	
2	Duality, partnership, opposition, balance, choice	
3	Trinity, mother/father/child, body/mind/spirit, creativity, growth, manifestation, joy, good fortune	
4	Stability, order, the material, earth, completeness, practicality, responsibility, circumscription	
5	Transformation, exploration, freedom, versatility, instability, quintessence, sensuality (five senses)	
6	Beauty, harmony, nurturance, sympathy, peace, the ideal	

NUMBER	ASSOCIATIONS	PERSONAL MEANINGS
7	Spirituality, mysticism, meditation, profound insight, psyche, magic, philosophy, the week	
8	Strength, lessons learned, hard work, achievement, goal orientation, resourcefulness, abundance	
9	Fulfillment, initiation, wholeness, selflessness	
10	End of a cycle, beginning of the next; completion; rebirth; over-ripeness; powerful leadership	
11	Master visionary, understanding spiritual truths, sensitivity, charisma	
12	Wisdom, life experience, ancient number of completion	
13	Unlucky, initiation, association with the flower of life	
22	The master builder, actualization of the divine within, serving the world in a practical way, idealism	
33	The master teacher and healer, spiritual uplifting of humanity, selfless service, Christ consciousness	
40	Trial, probation, initiation, death, wholeness	

body sense: getting in touch

If you have personal associations with any of these physical locations, they will prove more important to your interpretation than the common associations I've gathered here.

COMMON ASSOCIATIONS WITH PHYSICAL LOCATIONS

PHYSICAL LOCATION	ASSOCIATIONS	PERSONAL MEANINGS
Ankle	Steadiness, unsteadiness, "ankle-deep in something"	
Arm	Holding, hugging, empowering, acceptance ("with open arms"), companionship ("arm-in-arm")	
Back	Relating to your personal history, what is behind you, emotional support, protection, the unseen, annoyance, helplessness	
Belly	Nourishment, digestion, gestation, discontent ("to bellyache")	
Breast	Femininity, nurturance, inner nature ("bosom")	
Butt, buttocks	Sitting, walking, laughingstock ("butt of a joke"), intrusion ("butt in")	
Cheek	Youth ("rosy cheeks"), impudence	
Chest	Compassion, pride, breathing, revelation ("get something off your chest")	
Ear	Hearing, sound, attentiveness ("all ears")	
Elbow	Making space for yourself ("elbow someone out of the way"), prodding, work ("elbow grease")	
Eye	Vision, tears, vigilance ("keep your eyes peeled"), reprisal ("an eye for an eye"), surprise ("eye-opening")	
Face	Image, how you show yourself to the world, honor, self-respect ("to lose face"), confrontation ("face-to-face")	
Foot	Solidity, walk, embarrassment ("foot in mouth"), subservience ("at someone's feet")	

PHYSICAL LOCATION	ASSOCIATIONS	PERSONAL MEANINGS
Genitals	Sex, pleasure, passion, gender	
Hand	Action, handiness, holding on, grasping, labor, help, participation, possession ("get one's hands on")	
Head	Thinking, intuition, identity, calm, sanity	
Heart	Love, compassion, joy, courage, will, emotion	
Hip	Movement forward or to the side, handicap ("on the hip")	
Jaw	Chewing, resentment, determination ("to set your jaw")	
Knee	Bending, worship, submission, humility	
Leg	Travel, responsibility, power or lack of power ("not have a leg to stand on")	
Mouth	Eating, tasting, enjoying, speaking	
Muscle	Strength, movement, force	
Neck	Holding your head up, stubbornness, annoyance ("a pain in the neck"), keeping up with ("run neck-and-neck")	
Nose	Smelling, self-worth, obviousness ("as plain as the nose on your face"), inquisitiveness ("being nosy")	
Rectum	Elimination, letting go	
Shoulder	Carrying weight or a burden, cooperation ("shoulder to shoulder"), rejection ("cold shoulder")	
Spine	Strength of purpose, supporting yourself, determination ("to have backbone")	
Throat	Speaking, singing, swallowing	
Tooth	Decisiveness, chewing, irritation ("set your teeth on edge"), resoluteness ("tooth and nail")	
Torso	Vitality, the body as a whole	
Wrist	Flexibility, time ("wristwatch")	

acknowledgments

Many people helped me capture the flashes of inspiration that resulted in this book. My daughter Linnea Vedder sits atop this list. Not only did she create beautiful illustrations for our book, but her collaboration gave birth to my desire to write *The World Is Your Oracle*.

Again and again, my first reader, Ann Aswegan, reinforced my belief in the significance of this volume. As a kinesthetic diviner and dream expert, she also verified the value of these oracular types, which I might have doubted as an auditory person. I couldn't have had a better booster!

Farrell Collins was another early reader. As a procedural writer by profession, her help was invaluable when I created the structure of this book. Even more so, her love and support as my best buddy helped me "keep on keeping on." I miss her sorely.

My wonderful niece-in-law Madee Hartjes is a Jill of many trades. Her undergraduate degree was in biology, but it was her editing skills that improved many a paragraph in this book while she feted our family with foodie delights.

I also need to thank Elizabeth Matson. As the sole member of my "writers group" during an early part of my career, she nurtured my prose and appreciated my ideas. As a result, I never quit writing.

I also want to thank the participants in the divination classes I taught at the First Unitarian Society in Madison, Wisconsin, plus the CUUPs group there. As my first guinea pigs, they tested the earliest versions of *The World Is Your Oracle* and gave me positive feedback.

Gareth Esersky could not have been a more helpful literary agent. She supported me when the process became difficult, and most importantly, found Fair Winds Press to publish this book.

At Fair Winds, Jill Alexander believed in this book from the beginning. Her supportive guidance and insight helped shape this book, with the aid of Megan Buckley and Meredith Quinn, whose editorial advice fine-honed my prose.

And most importantly, I want to thank my husband Mark Shults. His love and support have been the ground upon which I built my work life. When it comes to this book, he discovered the scientific literature that gave rise to my chapter on "Science and Divination."

about the author

Nancy Vedder-Shults, Ph.D., is a storyteller, writer, and musician. The theological columnist for *SageWoman* magazine and blogger for *Tikkun Daily*, she has offered spiritual growth keynotes, workshops, and classes all over North America since 1987. Nancy honed her speaking and writing skills in the emerging field of Women's Studies from 1975 to 1991 at the University of Wisconsin-Madison. Her muse nudged her out of academia to record *Chants for the Queen of Heaven*. Check out her website at MamasMinstrel.net.